T0294650

CONTRACTORS IN THE GOVERNMENT WORKPLACE

Managing the Blended Workforce

Glenn J. Voelz

GOVERNMENT INSTITUTES

An imprint of
THE SCARECROW PRESS, INC.
Lanham • Toronto • Plymouth, UK
2010

Government Institutes

Published by Government Institutes
An imprint of The Scarecrow Press, Inc.
A wholly owned subsidiary of The Rowman & Littlefield Publishing Group, Inc.
4501 Forbes Boulevard, Suite 200, Lanham, Maryland 20706
www.govinstpress.com

Estover Road, Plymouth PL6 7PY, United Kingdom

Copyright © 2010 by Government Institutes

All rights reserved. No part of this book may be reproduced in any form or by any electronic or mechanical means, including information storage and retrieval systems, without written permission from the publisher, except by a reviewer who may quote passages in a review.

The reader should not rely on this publication to address specific questions that apply to a particular set of facts. The author and the publisher make no representation or warranty, express or implied, as to the completeness, correctness, or utility of the information in this publication. In addition, the author and the publisher assume no liability of any kind whatsoever resulting from the use of or reliance upon the contents of this book.

British Library Cataloguing in Publication Information Available

Library of Congress Cataloging-in-Publication Data

Voelz, Glenn J.
  Contractors in the government workplace : managing the blended workforce / Glenn J. Voelz.
    p. cm.
  Includes bibliographical references and index.
  ISBN 978-1-60590-698-0 (cloth : alk. paper)—ISBN 978-1-60590-699-7 (electronic)
  1. Government contractors—United States. 2. Administrative agencies—United States—Personnel management. I. Title.
  HD3861.U6V64 2010
  352.6—dc22

                                                                2009046821

∞ ™ The paper used in this publication meets the minimum requirements of American National Standard for Information Sciences—Permanence of Paper for Printed Library Materials, ANSI/NISO Z39.48-1992.

Printed in the United States of America

Contents

Preface

THE SIGNIFICANT EXPANSION of service-based contracting in the federal workplace has required that government managers possess greater knowledge of contract-administration practices and basic familiarity with the rules and regulations governing the operations of blended government-contractor workforces.

In most organizations there is no mandated training program or specialized preparatory material specifically designed to prepare nonacquisition-specialist supervisors to lead a mixed workforce of government and contract employees. As the government increasingly turns to commercial augmentation for an expanding variety of services, many closely supporting inherently governmental functions, it is critically important that supervisors understand the rules, expectations, and boundaries of the government-contractor relationship. Without an adequate understanding of basic contract oversight and administration best practices, supervisors run the risk of making unnecessary errors in their use of these contracted services.

It is important to remember that the government supervisor has many resources for assistance. In all cases, the contracting officer's representative (COR) should be the supervisor's first point of contact for any questions concerning the appropriate role, authorities, and functions of contractors in the government workplace. Contracting Officer's Representatives are required to complete mandatory training and continuing education in all aspects of contract management and administration. Furthermore, they are tasked with ensuring that all contracted services are delivered to the government according to standards specified in the contract language.

While the contracting officer and COR serve as an important resource for helping the supervisor with the challenges of managing the blended government-contractor team, the government's acquisition workforce is spread extremely thin and has not kept up growth with the massive expansion of service contracting in recent years. For this reason it is critical that government supervisors be sufficiently trained in the basics of contract administration and be familiar with the legal and ethical guidelines governing the use of contractors in their workplace. Effective contract management, administration, and oversight are a team effort, requiring the active participation of acquisition specialists as well as supervisors and employees. Only through a team approach will the government be assured of receiving good value and quality work from these commercial partnerships.

This handbook is designed to provide a basic introduction to contract administration best practices for nonacquisition specialists supervising the mixed government-contractor workforce. It describes the roles, authorities, and responsibilities of key players in the contract administration process and offers tips and guidance for supervisors to help them understand the government-contractor relationship and make the most effective use of commercial services.

Acknowledgments

THIS HANDBOOK IS BASED on extensive research of government-contracting regulations, manuals, training-program materials, acquisition publications, and profession periodicals. Additionally, I drew on personal experiences in managing blended government-contractor workforces as well as feedback gathered from group training seminars and interviews with experts in the field of government contracting and procurement. The majority of the publications, regulations, and documents referenced in this handbook are readily available in the public domain. Instances where excerpts, figures, quotations, and secondary-source materials are directly referenced or quoted in the text have been noted in the documentation. The handbook appendix also provides an extensive list of resources, web links, and background materials where additional information may be found. The views expressed in this handbook do not reflect the official policy or position of the Department of Defense or the U.S. Government.

1

Introduction and Handbook Overview

O VER THE PAST DECADE the federal government has experienced a massive expansion in its use of service contracting. In the Department of Defense (DOD) alone, spending on acquisition of commercial goods and services expanded to well over $314 billion annually.

The Background on Government-Service Contracting[1]

- The U.S. federal government is the single largest buyer of commercial services in the world. Each year federal agencies spend over $400 billion for a range of goods and services to satisfy mission needs.
- From fiscal year 2000 to fiscal year 2005, government purchasing of commercial goods and services increased nearly 75 percent.
- Between 1990 and 1995 the government began spending more on services than goods. Today, government spending on services accounts for more than 60 percent of total procurement dollars.

Understanding the Problem

This rapid increase in service contracting has exposed significant shortfalls in the government's oversight and contract-management procedures. The Government Accountability Office (GAO) has repeatedly identified government-contract management as a high-risk area vulnerable to fraud, waste, and misuse of taxpayer dollars.[2] The GAO found that vulnerability to these risks has been compounded by the rapid growth of federal contracting, significant shortfalls of trained acquisition personnel, and increasing demands for surveillance of service-based contracting.

These problems have been complicated by the government's growing reliance on contractors to perform many core-mission functions previously carried out by government personnel.[3] Many of these services closely support a variety of inherently governmental functions, such as acquisitions, intelligence, security, and program management. The use of commercial augmentation for these borderline inherently governmental functions requires increased scrutiny and oversight by government personnel in order to ensure the integrity of the government's decision-making process. Yet, habitual shortages of experienced acquisition specialists have left the government unprepared to fulfill its oversight responsibilities.

The government currently faces an acute shortage of federal-procurement professionals with between five and fifteen years of experience. This situation will only worsen, as roughly half of the current workforce becomes eligible for retirement in the next four years. Compounding these problems, the GAO has noted significant discrepancies in preparation and performance of contracting officers' representatives (COR), those individuals primarily tasked with conducting oversight and administrative functions for government-service contracts.

The expanded use of commercial augmentation, along with significant shortfalls of experienced contract-administration personnel, has left government agencies unable to provide adequate oversight and accountability for many of its contracted services. Numerous studies have revealed government-wide deficiencies in several key areas:

- challenges developing total workforce strategies and appropriate policies addressing which core governmental functions may be performed by commercial providers
- deficiencies in contract-administration procedures, scope of work infractions, conflict of interest problems, and habitual violations of Federal Acquisition Regulations
- lack of training for government and contractor personnel in the appropriate roles, responsibilities, and authorities in the blended government-contractor workplace
- inadequate consideration given to the risks of commercial sourcing for core governmental functions, as well as ethical and security concerns associated with employing contractors for certain sensitive functions
- poor oversight and surveillance of contractor performance

These problems, along with the enormous shortfall of experienced acquisition personnel, have left much of the burden of oversight and accountability to noncontracting-specialist supervisors and employees, many of whom are not trained in contracting regulations and procedures. Now, more than ever, all government employees and supervisors must understand contract-administration best practices and be familiar with rules and regulations governing the conduct of contractors in the workplace.

In most organizations there is no formal training program designed specifically to prepare nonacquisition government employees for supervisory roles in the mixed government-contractor workforce. As the government increasingly turns to commercial augmentation to satisfy myriad basic functions, it is critically important that all employees and leaders understand the rules, expectations, and boundaries of the government-contractor relationship. Active participation of government supervisors is integral to effective monitoring of contract performance, ensuring that contracted services are delivered on time, at cost, and according to quality standards specified in the contract language, as well as ensuring legal and ethical conduct of the blended workforce.

Handbook Overview

This handbook is intended to provide an introduction to the fundamentals of managing government-contractor relations in a blended workforce. It focuses primarily on issues relating to service-based contracting, the most rapidly expanding element of government acquisitions over the past decade. The handbook offers best practices and tips for employees and junior supervisors tasked with managing hybrid government-contractor teams.

This program is not designed for acquisition specialists, contracting officer representatives, program managers, or government employees with extensive professional experience leading mixed government-contractor workforces. Rather, the handbook is intended to provide an introductory-level overview of service-based contracting with a particular focus on improving supervisory techniques and management practices for mixed government-contractor teams.

Program Objectives

- to provide introduction to service-based contracting, contract types, and basic contracting terms, concepts, and references
- to provide an understanding of the government-contractor relationship and what each side contributes to the blended team
- to discuss performance-based service-acquisition methodologies, their effective application, and surveillance of these contract types

- to examine the responsibilities, authorities, and roles for each member of the acquisition team
- to develop a basic familiarity with the government's acquisition process, how contracts are developed, and the supervisor's role in facilitating effective contract administration and oversight
- to provide guidelines and tools for team building in a blended government-contractor workforce
- to offer strategies for analyzing operational processes in the blended workplace in order to increase efficiency in the use of commercial augmentation
- to offer tips for ethical, legal, and security considerations pertaining to the management of hybrid government-contractor workforces
- to identify and discuss how to avoid mistakes supervisors commonly make in managing hybrid government-contractor teams
- to develop tools and strategies for effective contract-surveillance methodologies, oversight techniques, and monitoring programs to evaluate and measure contractor performance

What This Handbook Does

- provides basic understanding of tools, techniques, rules, and regulations relating to the supervision of contractors in the workplace
- offers techniques for managing blended workforces, tips for team building, and guidelines for optimizing the performance of mixed government-contractor teams
- provides basic legal, ethical, and security tips to help avoid the common mistakes and violations of Federal Acquisition Regulation (FAR) guidelines

What This Handbook Does Not Do

- provide professional certification as an acquisition expert or contracting officer's representative (COR)
- train and qualify the reader to write contracts or make obligations on behalf of the government
- enable independent ethical or legal judgments on contractor activities or conduct in the workplace

Notes

1. Report of the Acquisition Advisory Panel, Office of Federal Procurement Policy and the United States Congress, January 2007.

2. GAO-08-621T, Defense Acquisitions: DOD's Increased Reliance on Service Contractors Exacerbates Long-Standing Challenges, April 3, 2008.

3. Government Accountability Office, DOD Needs to Reexamine Its Extensive Reliance on Contractors and Continue to Improve Management and Oversight, March 11, 2008.

2

Overview of Service-Based Contracting and Contract Types

Why the Government Uses Commercial Contracting

IDEALLY, CONTRACTING SHOULD OCCUR as the result of a deliberate and rationalized effort to satisfy a government need through a formal process of market research and competitive sourcing, seeking value for the taxpayer by leveraging the expertise and efficiency of commercial providers. In reality, there are often other reasons why contracting is used to satisfy temporary or long-term gaps in the government's workforce and productive process. In recent years the enormous expansion of government-service contracting has been utilized for several reasons:

1. to mitigate critical shortfalls of government personnel and fill short-term gaps in the civil service workforce
2. to satisfy an urgent need for unique, hard-to-find skill sets unavailable in the permanent government workforce
3. to satisfy short-term labor requirements in functional areas where the government, for various reasons, does not wish to hire full-time civil service personnel
4. to avoid congressionally mandated staffing limits for agencies, departments, and select government operations
5. as result of cost-benefit determinations whereby the use of commercial-sector augmentation is operationally or financially advantageous to the government

Understanding Government Outsourcing

Simply put, outsourcing is a decision by the government to purchase goods and services from an outside source. More specifically, it refers to

> the transfer of a support function traditionally performed by an in-house organization to an outside service provider. Outsourcing occurs in both the public and private sectors. While the outsourcing firm or government organization continues to provide appropriate oversight, the vendor is typically granted a degree of flexibility regarding how the work is performed. In successful outsourcing arrangements, the vendor utilizes new technologies and business practices to improve service delivery and/or reduce support costs. Vendors are usually selected as the result of a competition among qualified bidders.[1]

A closely related concept is *privatization,* which occurs when the government stops providing certain goods or services either by way of selling a government asset or operational capability, or by creating an agreement in which a government service is essentially franchised to commercial operators or government-sponsored corporations. In most cases privatization is meant to refer to the government contracting out to the commercial sector for procurement of goods and services.

Government outsourcing or privatization efforts have evolved significantly over the past thirty years as a mechanism intended to reduce the size, scope, and costs of the federal government and increase efficiency through private competition.

An Introduction to Service-Based Contracting

A *service contract* refers to a contract that directly engages the time and effort of a contractor whose primary purpose is to perform an identifiable task rather than to furnish a specific end item of supply.[2] It can cover services performed either by professional or nonprofessional personnel on an individual or organizational basis. Some of the more common areas in which service contracts are used follow:

- maintenance, overhaul, repair, servicing, rehabilitation, salvage, modernization, or modification of supplies, systems, or equipment
- routine recurring maintenance of real property
- housekeeping and facilities services
- professional advisory and assistance services
- operation of government-owned equipment, real property, and systems

- communications services
- architectural and engineering services
- transportation and related services
- research and development activities

A service contract may be either personal or nonpersonal in nature. In general, personal services are contracted activities that, in terms of contract or by the nature of administration, give the appearance that the contractor is a government employee. Except for certain specific circumstances outlined in the Federal Acquisition Regulation, the government generally does not contract for personal services. In simple terms, this means that the government generally does not hire contractors to be used interchangeably with government employees, nor should supervisors exercise the same control and management authority over contractor personnel as they would over a government employee.

To avoid potential problems with personal-services violations, government supervisors must remember to avoid conduct or actions that suggest the existence of an employer-employee relationship with contractor personnel. When in doubt, the litmus test question a supervisor should ask is, Does the performance of the contractor's assigned tasks require the exercise of continuous supervision, control, and direction on the part of the government supervisor? If the answer is yes, then it is possible that the contract is being administered in such a manner that could create the impression of personal services. This topic will be covered in greater detail later in the handbook.

Basic Concepts of Federal Contracting

This handbook is primarily intended to provide introductory management techniques for supervisors overseeing hybrid government-contractor workforces. The content focuses on developing a basic understanding of service-based contracting, tools for optimizing the function of the hybrid government-contractor team, and tips for ensuring that workplace activities are ethical, legal, and secure. Since the handbook is designed for non-acquisition specialists, it is not intended to make the reader an expert on federal-contracting regulations. Nevertheless, a basic level of knowledge of the acquisition process and contract-administration best practices is helpful for any supervisor leading mixed government-contractor teams.

This knowledge enables the supervisor to better communicate requirements and expectations to the government acquisition team, as well as to the vendor's site manager and employees. This base of knowledge will ensure that the hybrid workforce functions as an integrated team with common goals, expectations, and standards,ensuring that the government's requirements are satisfied in an ethical and efficient manner.

The next section is a general overview of key contracting concepts and terms. It is intended to familiarize government supervisors with the basic language of acquisitions. For guidance on specific policy and regulations, supervisors should always refer to subject matter experts in their agency, organizational legal office, or the Federal Acquisition Regulation (FAR).

The Government-Contracting Process

The government acquisition cycle is a multiphase process involving contract planning, development, and management. To some degree, supervisors may play a role in every stage of this process, offering their advice as subject matter experts and offering assistance to the contracting officer (CO) and COR to ensure the effective development and execution of the contract agreement. Below is an outline of the basic steps and requirements of the acquisition cycle.

Step 1: Contract Planning

- Determine the government's need.
- Analyze the requirements.
- Conduct market analysis.
- Complete source-selection planning.
- Develop solicitation terms, requirements. and conditions.

Step 2: Contract Development and Award

- Solicit offers.
- Evaluate bids.
- Negotiate with potential vendors.
- Award contract.

Step 3: Contract Management

- The vendor initiates work.
- Conduct contract-administration functions.
- Complete quality-assurance measures.
- Enact payment and accounting procedures.
- Close out or terminate the contract.

Understanding Government-Contract Types

It is not necessary that government supervisors and nonacquisition employees become experts in all technical details of various contract types. Nevertheless, a basic familiarity of key terminology and concepts is helpful in understanding how the government develops contracts for commercial services. The contract types outlined below have numerous variations and options that are beyond the scope of this handbook. The important point is that supervisors possess a general knowledge of the key terminology and contract types so that they can effectively communicate with the acquisition team and better understand the terms, conditions, and limitations of the contract language that apply to employees assigned to their team.

Generally speaking, there are two basic types of government contracts: cost reimbursement and fixed price.

Cost Reimbursement

Cost-reimbursement contracts place most risk on the government and are generally more burdensome to administer. These contracts are often used for projects involving some degree of technical or financial uncertainty or in cases where the exact costs of the contract cannot be accurately estimated. Some examples for use of this contract type are technical and expert services, research studies, investigative projects, or conceptual efforts in which the contractor's requirements or end-state deliverables cannot be reasonably priced. In these cases, the vendor's work is compensated on the basis of demonstrated level of effort rather than completion of a clearly specified task or enumerated end product. The contractor is expected to make a good-faith effort to meet the government's needs within an estimated cost for supply of goods and/or services. These contract types generally establish an initial cost estimate and ceiling that the contractor may not exceed without approval of the contracting officer.

The primary advantage of this contract type is that it provides greater flexibility than is generally possible under a fixed-price contract. But this contract type also carries maximum risk to the government, due to uncertainties in labor hours, the exact specifications of work to be completed, and the material and labor costs required. The government assumes nearly all risks of uncertainty when work cannot be completed within the expected cost or period of performance or if the work is not completed to standard. Additionally, the government assumes significant administrative and oversight burden and must exercise effective surveillance during the period of performance to ensure contractor efficiency, cost control, and delivery of the desired outcome.

A significant downside to this contract type is that it offers minimal incentives for the contractor to control costs; therefore, cost-reimbursement contracts are generally avoided except when uncertainties involved in contract performance do not permit costs to be estimated with sufficient accuracy to justify a fixed-price contract.

It is important to note that there are several variations of the cost-reimbursement contract, such as the cost-plus-fixed-fee contract in which the contractor receives reimbursement plus a predetermined fee. The fees are typically negotiated during the initial phase of the acquisition and may be tied to certain production goals or to a general scope of work or level of effort over a specified period of time when the end-state deliverable is indeterminate. Cost-reimbursement contracts may also be tied to incentive or award fees, where the contractor is compensated against set performance standards, efficiency measures, and/or demonstrated cost savings to the government. These contract types are intended to create incentives to encourage contractors to complete work on time and below cost estimates.

Fixed Price

While there are several types of fixed-price contracts, one of the most common is the basic firm-fixed-price contract. In this type, the contractor agrees to deliver all supplies or services, at the specified times, for an agreed price that cannot be changed without modifying the contract. Firm fixed-price contracts place maximum risk on the contractor and hold minimal risk for the government, since the contractor makes a commitment to deliver all goods or services in return for a fixed payment. If the contractor fails to deliver the goods or services at the agreed price, they potentially become liable for any cost overruns or for a breach of contract.

Because the burden of risk is placed on the contractor rather than the government, there is a great incentive for the contractor to seek efficiency, lower costs, and satisfy delivery requirements, since they incur the burden of default. Hence, such a contract generally reduces the government's administrative and monitoring obligation more so than with cost-reimbursement contracts.

While these contract types have clear benefits for the government, there are situations in which they cannot be used due to uncertainties or ambiguities in costs or delivery requirements. In cases where the contractor cannot develop a reliable cost estimate or assured delivery standard, they will often not be willing to run the risk of agreeing to a fixed-price contract. For this reason it is difficult to apply fixed-price contracts to certain types of activities such as conceptual projects, research-and-development efforts, or other tasks where price and risk cannot be easily assessed beforehand.

Summary of Basic Contract Types

The chart below (table 2.1) provides general descriptions of the more common variations of the basic types of government contracts. This list in not exhaustive but does provide some explanation of the various contract types and principle characteristics, as well as other common acquisition methods such as indefinite-delivery contracts and blanket purchase agreements. Government supervisors managing a hybrid workforce should be generally aware of the terminology, characteristics, and function of each type. This information will help supervisors better understand the terms and conditions of the contractors providing services in their workplace.

The Federal Acquisition Regulation (FAR)

The Federal Acquisition Regulation codifies basic government policies for acquisition of supplies and services by executive agencies. It is the principal set of rules and regulations defining the acquisition process, including service contracting. The FAR outlines procedural steps, rules for planning and developing of contracts, and the process of contract administration. The FAR also regulates the activities of government personnel involved in the acquisition process, including the conduct of supervisors and government employees working as part of a hybrid workforce.

While it is not necessary that government employees or supervisors become experts in every detail of the FAR, it is important that they possess a basic understanding of the purpose and scope of the regulation, as well as how it relates to the conduct of their professional activities in the workplace. It is a useful reference for interpreting the technical language of many government contracts as it contains standard clauses that are incorporated into many government contracts and references relating to the solicitation process and activities of contractors.

The FAR was developed with a number of guiding principles designed to facilitate the government's procurement of commercial items and services. The general scope of these objectives is outlined below:

- Provide an acquisition system that satisfies customers' needs in terms of cost, quality, and timeliness.
- Minimize administrative operating costs.
- Conduct business with integrity, fairness, and openness.
- Fulfill other public-policy objectives, such as socioeconomic requirements and national sourcing goals and priorities.

Contract Type	Description	Usage and Application	Obligation of the Contractor	Risks to the Government	Potential Issues
Firm Fixed Price	Suitable for acquiring commercial items, supplies or services with well-defined specifications, delivery schedules and cost estimates. Price is not subject to adjustment without modification of the contract.	Used primarily when government's requirement is well defined and the contractor can reasonably estimate cost, time, materials and the level of effort required.	Provide an acceptable standard of delivery at the fixed time, place and price specified in the contract.	Low risk to the government. The contractor assumes all cost risk for performing the work at the agreed price and standard.	Contractors should be experienced in the type of work and able to accurately estimate costs and delivery timelines. Market conditions should be stable to reduce the risk of cost overrun or default.
Fixed-Price Economic Price Adjustment	A fixed price with formula for adjusting certain payments based on variations due to market changes, actual labor or material costs.	Used to help mitigate risk to the contractor due to uncertainty in markets for material or labor. Often used for long-term acquisitions of commercial supplies or services.	Provide an acceptable standard of delivery at the fixed time, place and price specified in the contract with allowance for economic adjustment.	Slightly higher risk to the government based on fluctuations in labor or material prices. Generally not used unless absolutely necessary to protect the contractor against price fluctuations.	Requires greater justification for use according to contracting regulations. Must have a clear, mutually agreed basis for determining any potential cost adjustments.

Table 2.1. Basic contract types.

Contract Type	Description	Usage and Application	Obligation of the Contractor	Risks to the Government	Potential Issues
Fixed Price Level of Effort	A fixed-price for a specified level of effort by the contractor over a stated period of time.	Used for technical and expert services such as investigations, research and development projects, or other conceptual work where results are achieved through application of specified type of effort rather than a finite product.	Level of effort performance at the time, place, and the price fixed in the contract.	Contractor is only required to provide a level of effort rather than delivery of a clearly specified outcome. Contractor is incentivized to maximize chargeable hours and extend the life of the contract.	Requires a clear methodology for evaluating the contractor's performance against measureable standards. Difficult to measure the value returned to government and to define acceptable standards of delivery.
Cost Plus Fixed Fee	A cost-reimbursement contract for payment of a negotiated fee above the actual costs determined at the start of the contract.	For technical and expert services, research studies, investigative efforts or conceptual efforts where requirements are relatively uncertain or cannot be reasonably priced.	Contractor is expected to make a good faith effort to meet the government's needs within an estimated cost for goods or services.	Maximum risk to government due to uncertainties in labor hours, type of work and material required to perform the contract. The government assumes the risk when work cannot be completed within the expected cost or time.	The government must exercise significant surveillance during performance to ensure the use of efficient methods, cost controls and delivery of desired outcomes. There are minimal incentives for the contractor controlling costs.

(continued)

Contract Type	Description	Usage and Application	Obligation of the Contractor	Risks to the Government	Potential Issues
Time and Materials	For services or supplies provided at a specified fixed hourly rate on the basis of direct labor and material costs.	Used only when no other contract types are suitable. Frequently used for emergency repair, technical services, or maintenance work.	Contractor is expected to make a good faith effort to meet the government's needs within an agreed ceiling price.	Maximum risk to government. Contractor is rewarded for inefficiency as more hours worked mean more profit. The government assumes all risk if work cannot be completed on time or within cost estimates.	Labor rates must be negotiated in advance. Provides no incentive for the contractor to control costs or seek efficiencies. Government must exercise significant surveillance to monitor efficiency, quality, and value.
Indefinite Delivery Contract Types	Three types: Definite-Quantity contracts, Requirement contracts, and Indefinite-Quantity contracts. All may be used to acquire supplies or services when the exact time and/or quantity of future deliveries are unknown. Also known as Task Orders (for services) and Delivery Orders (for supplies).	Used when the government cannot predetermine the precise quantity of supplies or services required over a fixed period of time. Often used for maintaining supply stocks, basic services, architectural or engineering services.	Contractor performs services or deliveries of goods at the time, place, and prices fixed in the contract.	Contracts usually limit the government's obligation to minimum and/or maximum quantities and/or dollar amounts specified in the contract.	Provides the government maximum flexibility to satisfy uncertain, short-term requirements for basic services and supplies.

Table 2.1. (*continued*)

Contract Type	Description	Usage and Application	Obligation of the Contractor	Risks to the Government	Potential Issues
Blanket Purchase Agreement	A simplified acquisition method used to fill repetitive needs for supplies or services. BPAs can be established under the GSA Schedules Programs to provide streamlined and simplified acquisitions.	Used to procure a wide variety of items in a broad class of supplies or services when the exact items, quantities, and delivery requirements are not known in advance or are subject to considerable variation.	Delivery of goods and services in accordance with the agreed with the GSA schedule program. Offers benefits to both the government and the vendor by minimizing administrative requirements.	A standing BPA does not obligate the government to place any orders, nor does it obligate the vendor to accept them but one a BPA order is accepted, an enforceable contract is created.	Vendors should have a dependable record of past performance, quality of services and competitive prices. BPAs for hourly rate services still require a Statement of Work.

It is important to remember that the FAR not only applies to the functions of acquisition teams and conduct of government employees. Commercial bidders must also comply with the provisions and guidelines of the FAR in order to be awarded government contracts.

With regard to service-based acquisitions, FAR part 37 applies to all contracts regardless of the type of contract or service. Below is an outline of the FAR general structure and major subparts:

Subchapter A: General
    Part 1: Federal Acquisition Regulations System
    Part 2: Definitions of Words and Terms
    Part 3: Improper Business Practices and Personal Conflicts of Interest
    Part 4: Administrative Matters
Subchapter B: Competition and Acquisition Planning
    Part 5: Publicizing Contract Actions
    Part 6: Competition Requirements
    Part 7: Acquisition Planning
    Part 8: Required Sources of Supplies and Services
    Part 9: Contractor Qualifications
    Part 10: Market Research
    Part 11: Describing Agency Needs
    Part 12: Acquisition of Commercial Items
Subchapter C: Contracting Methods and Contract Types
    Part 13: Simplified Acquisition Procedures
    Part 14: Sealed Bidding
    Part 15: Contracting by Negotiation
    Part 16: Types of Contracts
    Part 17: Special Contracting Methods
    Part 18: Emergency Acquisitions
Subchapter D: Socioeconomic Programs
    Part 19: Small-Business Programs
    Part 20: [RESERVED, not currently in use]
    Part 21: [RESERVED, not currently in use]
    Part 22: Application of Labor Laws to Government Acquisitions
    Part 23: Environment, Energy and Water Efficiency, Renewable Energy Technologies, Occupational Safety, and Drug-Free Workplace
    Part 24: Protection of Privacy and Freedom of Information
    Part 25: Foreign Acquisition
    Part 26: Other Socioeconomic Programs
Subchapter E: General Contracting Requirements
    Part 27: Patents, Data, and Copyrights

Part 28: Bonds and Insurance
Part 29: Taxes
Part 30: Cost-Accounting Standards Administration
Part 31: Contract Cost Principles and Procedures
Part 32: Contract Financing
Part 33: Protests, Disputes, and Appeals
Subchapter F: Special Categories of Contracting
Part 34: Major System Acquisition
Part 35: Research-and-Development Contracting
Part 36: Construction and Architect-Engineer Contracts
Part 37: Service Contracting
Part 38: Federal Supply-Schedule Contracting
Part 39: Acquisition of Information Technology
Part 40: [RESERVED, not currently in use]
Part 41: Acquisition of Utility Services
Subchapter G: Contract Management
Part 42: Contract Administration and Audit Services
Part 43: Contract Modifications
Part 44: Subcontracting Policies and Procedures
Part 45: Government Property
Part 46: Quality Assurance
Part 47: Transportation
Part 48: Value Engineering
Part 49: Termination of Contracts
Part 50: Extraordinary Contractual Actions and the Safety Act
Part 51: Use of Government Sources by Contractors
Subchapter H: Clauses and Forms
Part 52: Solicitation Provisions and Contract Clauses
Part 53: Forms

Office of Management and Budget's (OMB) Revised Circular A-76

Another document that supervisors will hear frequently referenced is the Office of Management and Budget's (OMB) Revised Circular A-76. The present incarnation of the circular is the culmination of twenty years' effort aimed at reforming the federal government's system for procurement of goods and services. The major movement for reform began under the Reagan administration and continued through the Clinton administration's National Performance Review (NPR).

OMB A-76 sets forth the policies and procedures that executive-branch agencies must use in identifying commercial-type activities and in determining whether these activities are best provided by the private sector, government employees, or other government agencies through a fee-for-service agreement. This process is often referred to as *competitive sourcing.* Additionally, the circular establishes federal policy regarding performance of commercial activities and implements related statutory requirements.

The fundamental premise of the A-76 process is based on several key assumptions:[3]

- that the federal government should not compete against its citizens and rely on the commercial sector to supply its products and services
- that the government can conduct cost-comparison studies and use managed competitions to determine the best provider for these goods and services
- that market forces will determine the most effective and cost-efficient methods to operate both governmental and commercial functions
- that fair and open marketplace competition will reduce requirements for government oversight

The overall aim of these initiatives is to improve government efficiency and performance by requiring federal agencies to identify noninherently governmental activities and then conduct managed competitions to determine who can best perform the service—either the government or the private sector. The government's purpose in these efforts is threefold:

- to achieve economy and enhance productivity in government services
- to retain governmental functions in-house that are inherently governmental in nature
- to rely on commercially available sources for products and services whenever practical and in those cases when a product or service can be procured more economically from a commercial source

One of the basic functions of A-76 is to define federal policies for determining which recurring activities should be transferred to the private sector and which the government should retain. As part of this, A-76 provides general guidelines for identifying "inherently governmental" functions that should not be subject to commercial competition. Once these determinations are made, the circular provides the government's basic methodology for determining the most economical means of subjecting these activities to a competitive process with private-sector providers. To this end, A-76 outlines the steps for conducting cost-comparison studies to determine optimal sourcing solutions and a process for managing private-sector competition for federal contracts. The policy requires the government to prepare competing cost estimates based on the price of performing the same work using government employees to determine the best alternative. These procedures are designed to subject designated governmental activities to the forces of competition, thereby ensuring that taxpayers receive maximum value, efficiency, and benefit for their tax dollars.

Perhaps the most critical aspect of the competitive-sourcing process is the government's clear articulation of the type of work to be performed and the desired outcome. This process must take place before accurate cost estimates can be derived and offers can be solicited from the private sector. The next section describes the government's basic strategy for defining requirements and applying performance-based service-acquisition methodologies to optimize public-private partnerships.

Performance-Based Service Acquisition (PBSA)

Performance-based service acquisition (PBSA) involves strategies, methods, and techniques for articulating the government's needs as measurable outcomes rather than as specific performance processes. PBSA is structured around defining service requirements in terms of general performance objectives with the intent of offering potential commercial providers the latitude to determine how best to satisfy the government's needs.

Most experienced government supervisors are likely familiar with the traditional contracting statement of work (SOW) method that offers a detailed description of process requirements and performance standards expected from the contractor. One of the major distinctions with PBSA methodology is how the performance work statement (PWS) is developed and implemented, saddling the contractor with primary responsibility for determining how a given objective is accomplished, rather than requiring the government to specify exactly how the work will be done.

According to the FAR, all executive departments are expected to use PBSA methodologies to the maximum extent possible when acquiring services. For this reason, it is important that government supervisors be familiar with PBSA methodology as the government moves toward greater utilization of these strategies for service-based contracting.

While the PBSA methodology offers numerous advantages in terms of permitting the contractor increased flexibility and leverage in devising efficient solutions to achieve the government's goals, it also presents challenges for acquisition teams in terms of ensuring that desired outcomes are clearly defined, that standards and objectives are understood by the contractor, and that the objectives are fully satisfied.

With performance-based acquisitions, supervisors and other government subject matter experts play an important role in the contract-development process, assisting the acquisition team in defining requirements and describing desired outcomes. For this reason, it is critical that supervisors possess a basic understanding of the PBSA methodology and how it affects the operation of mixed government-contractor workforces.

The key to performance-based contracting is structuring the acquisition development process around the purpose of the work to be performed and desired outcomes rather than the specific steps of a process. To be effective, government requirements should be established in clear, specific, and objective terms with measurable outcomes. The process does not require specific detailed instructions as to how the work will be performed by the contractor. Devising optimal process solutions is left up to the expertise and innovation of the commercial provider, permitting them to seek the most efficient solution to achieve the desired outcome at an agreed price and standard of quality.

Objectives of Performance-Based Service Acquisitions

By focusing on performance outcomes rather than simply describing how the contractor will perform their work, the government hopes to achieve numerous benefits over the traditional statement-of-work methodology. PBSA methodology is designed to achieve several key objectives:

- Maximize performance by permitting the contractor to deliver a required service using its own best practices and innovative solutions. Focus is on the end result and desired outcomes rather than process, enabling contractors to continually adjust and optimize their operations without requiring contract modification.
- Incentivize contractor performance by encouraging vendors to seek innovation and efficiencies in their processes while achieving the government's desired end state. Contracts may be developed to reward contractor-developed solutions resulting in cost savings and time and labor efficiency.
- Maximize competition and innovation by using performance requirements rather than government-directed processes. Use of innovative commercial-sector solutions will also offer the benefit of attracting a broader base of industry providers with a variety of experience and expertise.

- Encourage and promote the use of commercial-sector services and productive standards by reducing government-only contract clauses and similar requirements, thereby reducing the burden for management and oversight.
- Shift risk from the government to industry as contractors become responsible for achieving objectives through the use of proprietary best practices and processes.

Desired Benefits of Performance-Based Service Acquisitions

Ideally, when these contract vehicles are developed and executed in an efficient manner, there are numerous benefits that may be achieved:

- increased likelihood of achieving mission needs and desired outcomes
- focus on results and outcomes, not process
- better value and enhanced performance
- less performance risk to the government
- less requirement for detailed specifications and process description
- contractor flexibility in proposing optimal solutions
- Better competition and improved range of solutions
- contractor buy-in and shared interests in outcomes
- incentives promote innovation and cost-effectiveness
- less likelihood of a successful protest
- surveillance that is less frequent and more meaningful
- variety of solutions from which to choose

Basic Elements of the Performance-Based Service Acquisitions Process

The government identifies several basic elements common to all performance-based service acquisition processes.

- *Performance work statement.* This describes the government's desired outcomes in terms of measurable standards rather than prescriptive instructions.
- *Measurable performance standards.* These are standards for measuring the contractor's performance as well as the methodology for assessing contractor performance against those standards.
- *Performance-assessment plan.* This describes how contractor performance will be measured and assessed against performance standards.
- *Remedies.* Such procedures address how performance will be managed and actions taken when outcomes do not meet the specified performance

standards. Incentives should be used, where appropriate, to encourage performance that will exceed standards.

Steps of Performance-Based Service Acquisitions

There are seven basic steps of the PBSA process. While government supervisors are not expected to be involved in every stage of the acquisition process, it is important to note that input of subject matter experts is critical in several steps of the overall process.

- Establish the acquisition team.
- Describe the problem and outline the government's need.
- Examine various private-sector and public-sector solutions.
- Develop performance work statement (PWS) or statements of objective (SOO).
- Determine how to measure and manage performance.
- Select the right contractor.
- Manage performance and ensure delivery.

How the Government Supervisor Comes into Play

> The acquisition team consists of all participants in government acquisition, including not only representatives of the technical, supply, and procurement communities but also the customers they serve and the contractors who provide the products and services.[4]

Prior to the current emphasis on performance-based contracting, it was not uncommon for acquisition teams to work in relative isolation from the requiring activity. This situation inevitably resulted in ineffective surveillance methodologies, unmanageable administration, and poorly written work statements that were misaligned with the government's needs. Even more so than with traditional contracting methodologies, the PBSA process demands that the acquisition team draws on the experience and perspective of subject matter experts in the development and execution of service contracts. Supervisors, project managers, and government employees are critical stakeholders in this process, since they are the ones who will work most closely with the contractor team at the site of performance.

Service contracts are notoriously difficult to write—in part because contracting officers and CORs are often not functional experts on the particular technical aspects of the requirements being written into the contract. While acquisition specialists have significant experience with contract development, they often lack intimate knowledge and experience with the technical details of the actual tasks being performed by the contractor. As a result, traditional contract statements of work often fail to reflect the actual nature of government's needs, particularly the detailed performance requirements defining a satisfactory outcome.

Government service contracts are habitually inadequate in terms of establishing effective surveillance methodologies, as well as defining clear and measurable performance metrics. This situation inevitably results in contractors being paid for showing up and offering a vaguely defined effort rather than returning measurable results and good value to the government. This is arguably the single greatest problem with government service contracting in recent years.

The challenge of developing detailed and instructive descriptions of desired outcomes is particularly daunting with the expanding use of performance-based service acquisitions, which, by their nature, emphasize requirements in terms of general performance objectives rather than the specific process descriptions. Development of effective performance work statements can be extremely challenging even for experienced contracting experts. For this reason, PBSA methodology requires close involvement of all players during the development process, including supervisors, subject matter experts, customers, and users, as well as industry representatives when appropriate. This team should be involved throughout the acquisition cycle, particularly during the requirements analysis, market-research phase, contract-development process, administration, and evaluation.

While the acquisition team is ultimately responsible for the final terms of the contract, government supervisors may offer important contributions assisting the contracting officer and COR with development of requirements language, steps of the administration processes, surveillance methodologies, and advice on day-to-day direction and supervision of contract execution. This close partnership is critical for ensuring that the service contract is administered in a manner that is legal, ethical, and efficient and that adheres to all applicable regulations.

It is important for supervisors to remember that in a typical government workforce there are numerous individuals likely to have important contributions to offer the acquisition team. It is the responsibility of the government supervisor to leverage the experience and knowledge of their workforce to assist in the development phase to ensure that the final results of the contract accurately reflect the needs of the government and the actual nature of the work to be performed. Although not formally part of the acquisition team, several individuals may play critical roles in this process:

- *Government manager or supervisor.* In many cases the government supervisor may act as the primary subject matter expert for the requiring activity. Among the entire acquisition team, the supervisor is most likely to have extensive knowledge of the overall workflow process, guidelines, regulations, and detailed process specifications for the work that a prospective contractor will be expected to perform. The supervisor will also understand the challenges and limitations that the contractor team will face and can ensure that all relevant issues are presented in the requirements language.
- *Technical specialist or program manager.* The input of various technical experts, knowledgeable about the specific aspects of the performance requirements, is critical to the development of an effective performance-based contract. These individuals are typically most familiar with the technical requirements and can identify potential tradeoffs and shortfalls, judge the viability of a contractor's proposal, and assess whether a particular vendor is capable of providing the service. Since the contracting officer and COR will likely not possess expertise in the specific technical aspects of the work, they will need the help of technical specialists to conduct effective market research, requirements analysis, proposal evaluation, and contract development. These contributions are critical for ensuring that the performance work statement accurately reflects the government's needs and that the proper vendor is selected.
- *Customer or end user.* There is great value in soliciting input from the intended end consumer of the prospective contractor's effort. Ultimately, the success or failure of the contractor's effort should be judged on the utility and satisfaction offered to the consumer of the contractor's product or service. Unfortunately, this type of end-state focused input is often neglected during the acquisition process. Time constraints, as well as the challenge of effectively quantifying user inputs, makes the integration of this type of information difficult to achieve. Nevertheless, the acquisition team must always keep in mind the needs of the final customer and the perspective of government employees who will be working side by side with the contractor. These individuals can provide invaluable insight to help refine the requirement statement, assess potential risks, define specifications and articulate the required quality standards needed by the end user. The government employee working at the site of performance and the end consumer of the contractor's service will also be able to identify unseen trade-offs or shortfalls that may occur from using a commercial provider.

Conducting the Performance-Requirement Analysis

One of the key areas in which supervisors, technical experts, and end customers can make important contributions to the acquisition process is during the requirements-analysis phase. Unlike traditional SOW methodologies in which the government tells the contractor precisely how to do the work, the essence of the performance-based approach is describing requirements as outcomes rather than processes. For this reason it is critical that the contract performance work statement clearly articulate a detailed description of the government's requirement. This demands a systematic approach to analyzing the government's need in order to develop a detailed description of the desired outcome.

Below are the basic elements of the performance-requirement analysis. Supervisors, technical experts, and end customers all have important contributions to offer during each stage of this process.

- *Define the desired outcomes.* Determine what must be accomplished in order to satisfy the government's need.
- *Conduct outcome analysis.* Identify specific, measurable performance objectives, sequential milestones, and tasks that must be accomplished to arrive at the desired outcome.
- *Conduct performance analysis.* Identify performance standards and acceptable quality levels for delivery.

Conducting a Supervisor's Operational Analysis

In order for a supervisor or technical subject matter expert to offer a meaningful contribution to the performance-requirement analysis, they must first have a clear understanding of the elemental processes of their workplace. This analysis will enable the supervisor to describe to the acquisition team how the contractor's service will be integrated into their operation and best contribute to the achievement of the government's overall goals.

Even if a contract is already in place, it is still valuable for supervisors to conduct a detailed operational analysis of their organization's mission, requirements, and resources. This information will enable supervisors to make better operational and resourcing decisions, increase efficiency of their processes, and optimize their integration and utilization of commercial augmentation.

The basic techniques for conducting operation analysis will be familiar to most government supervisors trained in any type of deliberate planning

processes. Most government organizations have similar systems for conducting internal analysis and review. While some of the questions below
may seem very basic, the process is a necessary and useful exercise, assisting
supervisors in identifying organizational deficiencies and optimizing their
use of available resources—including contractor support.

Begin this process by asking some basic questions about the operation of
the government organization:

1. What is the organization required to do? What is the mission statement? What are the specified and implied subtasks required to accomplish the core mission functions?
2. What are the key policy documents, regulations, laws, and guidelines
   that define the structure, operation, and processes of the organization?
3. What specific goods, services, or outputs must be produced by the organization? Which of these tasks are mandated, which are implied, and
   which are simply done "because that's the way we've always done it"?
4. Are there ongoing tasks, requirements, or processes that are tangential
   to the core mission functions? Should these requirements be modified
   or eliminated?
5. What are the standards of quality or the production specifications
   defining the output of the organization's goods or services? How are
   these standards measured? What are the quantitative and qualitative
   measures of production that define success for the organization?
6. What external rules, regulations, or policies impact or constrain the
   delivery of the organization's goods or services?
7. What resources enable the organization's process? Consider such factors as funding, manpower, technology, use of commercial augmentation, and collaboration with external partners.
8. What are the variables, controlled and uncontrolled, that potentially
   impact the organization's operations? Consider such issues as regulatory, environmental, or budgetary changes. If possible, list the operative assumptions that underlie the selected variables. While not all
   variables may be anticipated, identifying basic assumptions will help
   supervisors gear their organizations for adjustments when required.
9. What are the human-capital resources necessary to accomplishing the
   organization's required tasks? Consider such issues as personnel skill
   sets, workforce-training needs, augmentation by external specialists,
   use of nongovernmental resources, and outside contractors.
10. What are the major constraints and limitations inhibiting the achieve-
    ment of desired outcomes? Restraints may be material needs, financial

or budgetary constraints, labor or human-capital shortfalls, limitations of systems capabilities and technology, deficiencies in personnel training, regulatory constraints, managerial deficiencies, or others.

11. Are there tasks, services, or outputs that should be accomplished but are not being achieved due to resource or other limitations?
12. Are the available resources properly aligned to enable the organization to satisfy its required mission tasks?
13. Is the organization properly structured and organized to satisfy its required mission tasks?
14. Is the productive process of the organization optimized for efficiency and full utilization of all available resources?

Once this basic analysis is complete, the supervisor should then consider how the work of the contractor (on hand or projected) fits into the picture. Ideally, if a contract is already in place these considerations should have been taken into account during the performance-requirements analysis phase of the initial acquisition. Unfortunately, the reality for many government organizations is that contractor support is all too often poorly planned, underutilized, inefficiently employed, or assigned to tasks and requirements differing significantly from the original intent and design of the acquisition. In many cases, responsibility for fixing these problems and optimizing the use of contractor support falls to the cooperative efforts of the government supervisor and COR. This is not how it should work but in reality often does.

To a certain degree such problems are inevitable due to the fact that government mission requirements are dynamic. Oftentimes, modifications to a contract's requirements statement or scope of work will lag behind the changing operational demands of an organization. This situation necessitates that supervisors continually make minor adjustments to their internal workflow process and organizational structure to ensure that contractor support is optimized just as they would for any other resource input.

In theory, use of PBSA methodology should resolve some of these problems by focusing contractor support on outcomes rather than processes. Performance-based contracting should permit the contractor to identify necessary adjustments in processes and to make these changes in order to achieve optimal efficiency without requiring a rewrite of the contract statement of work. Supervisors can play a positive role in facilitating this process by conducting a detailed operational analysis, which provides the acquisition team with a full understanding of all inputs into the organizational process, including the capabilities and limitations of the contractor workforce.

Determining How the Contractor Fits into the Process

Once the supervisor conducts an operational analysis of their organization, they must then determine how best to integrate and use contractor support. If a new contract is being developed, the supervisor may conduct this process as part of the formal performance-requirements analysis. But even if a contract is already in place, there is still great benefit derived from conducting a formal review of how contractor support is presently being utilized within the organization. If deficiencies or shortcomings are discovered, supervisors can use the results of this analysis to work with the contracting officer, the COR, and the vendor's site manager in order to optimize the employment of contractor support. When considering how this support may be most effectively employed, several questions should be considered:

1. What does the organization require of the contractor workforce? Identify factors such as man-hours, tasks, expertise, and knowledge that may be leveraged to mitigate gaps in the government's workforce or processes. Consider unique vendor services, skills, or resources that the government can apply to improve its process.
2. What are the potential factors limiting the use of contractor support? Consider such factors as budgetary constraints, manpower limitations, shortfalls in contractor skills or training, adverse impacts of market conditions such as labor or material costs, or lack of systems and technology available for contractor use.
3. Will the acquisition process provide the required support within an acceptable time frame to satisfy the government's needs? What are the costs and operational risks involved in waiting for the acquisition process to deliver the requested services?
4. To what aspects of the organization's process can contractors contribute? If a contract is currently in place, consider the limitations of the existing statement of work. Are all tasks or services required by the government accurately reflected within the existing scope of work?
5. If a contract is in place, does the current language need to be modified in order to satisfy ongoing or projected operational needs?
6. Does the organization possess adequate resources to properly monitor and evaluate the contractor's performance? Is there a need for additional government supervisors or contracting officer's technical representatives (COTR) to ensure effective surveillance?
7. Given the tasks currently assigned to the contractor workforce, are standards of delivery and quality of output adequately measured and assessed?

8. Can the efficiency of the organization's workflow process be quantified and easily measured? How can the contractor's contribution to this process be assessed? What are the measures used to determine the contractor's efficiency? Is the contractor doing a sufficient job monitoring their own quality standards and taking steps to improve efficiency?

9. What policies, regulations, or legal limitations apply to the use of contractor support in the workplace? Consider any potential factors limiting the contractor's ability to perform certain tasks, such as constraints imposed by the contract language, prohibitions against contractors performing inherently governmental functions, potential personal-services concerns, and security restrictions limiting contractor access to sensitive information.

10. What are the potential risks and liabilities of employing contractor support? Consider legal liabilities, security concerns, and safety issues, particularly for contractors deployed in support of contingency operations.

Notes

1. Department of Defense, Office of the Undersecretary of Defense for Acquisition and Technology. *Report of the Defense Science Board, Task Force on Outsourcing and Privatization.* August 1996. p. 7a.

2. FAR subpart 37.101.

3. For a useful overview of the circular see, Congressional Research Service Report for Congress, *Defense Outsourcing: The OMB Circular A-76 Policy,* June 30, 2005.

4. FAR 1.102(c).

3

Functions of the
Government-Contractor Team
Roles, Responsibilities, and Authorities

Roles, Responsibilities, and Authorities of the Acquisition Team

THIS CHAPTER PROVIDES a general outline of the duties, responsibilities, and expectations for each member of the acquisition team. It is intended to help the government supervisor understand the players who will assist them in achieving a successful outcome from the government-contractor partnership. For specific legal definitions and responsibilities, always refer to the Federal Acquisitions Regulation.

The Role of the Contracting Officer (CO)

By law, the contracting officer is an individual duly appointed with authority to enter into contracts on behalf of the U.S. government. In simple terms, this means that he or she is the government's authorized agent for all dealings and negotiations with the vendor. The CO has sole authority to solicit proposals, to negotiate terms of agreement, and to award and modify contracts on behalf of the government. In order to fulfill these functions, the CO requires assistance from a variety of technical, administrative, and legal advisors who help develop and administer of the contract.

Supervisor's Interactions with the Contracting Officer

Generally speaking, government supervisors will have relatively limited contact with contracting officers (CO). In the vast majority of situations the contracting officer's representative (COR) will be the supervisor's primary point of contact for issues relating to execution of the contract. Nevertheless, it is important for government supervisors dealing directly with contractor employees to understand the duties, authorities, and responsibilities of the contracting officer as well as the other players involved in the contract administration process.

In some circumstances the contracting officer may be far removed from the site of performance with limited oversight of the day-to-day services performed by the contractor. In such situations a contracting officer's representative will typically be appointed and colocated at the site of performance. This individual should be familiar with the specifics of the contractor's daily operations and act on behalf of the contracting officer for designated contract-administrative functions. In many cases where highly technical functions or specialized services are being performed, the CO and the COR may lack training or experience in the particular area of the contractor's work. For this reason, the government supervisor plays an important role assisting the acquisition team as a subject-matter expert. The supervisor may offer significant advice and assistance relating to the organizational process, standards of performance, skill requirements for contractor personnel, or details concerning the government's needs and requirements. The supervisor may also play a role assisting the CO and COR in various administration and surveillance functions, facilitating inspections and with various contract oversight responsibilities.

The CO and COR ultimately bear responsibility for the development, execution, and oversight of the contract, but the supervisor plays an important role ensuring effective administration by nature of their close day-to-day involvement with the workforce. The supervisor likely possesses significant knowledge and experience concerning the government's requirements and processes, making their input crucial to a successful acquisition process. This input is also extremely valuable during the contract development phase with such tasks as preparing contract-requirements statements, assisting with market research, providing technical contributions to requests for proposal, and other functions of contract administration. Since the supervisor is a critical contributor to this process, it is important that they possess at least a general understanding of contract-administration functions, as well as the roles, authorities, and responsibilities of the contracting officer and other members of the acquisition team.

Duties of the Contracting Officer

1. The contracting officer (CO or KO) is responsible for overall contract-administrative oversight, including establishing the terms and condi-

tions of delivery and ensuring that the vendor satisfies all stated requirements of the contract.

2. The CO is the primary authority responsible for safeguarding the interests of the United States government in contractual relationships.

3. The CO is responsible for conducting contract negotiations with the vendor on behalf of the government.

4. During the initial stages of the acquisition process, the CO reviews the requirements of the requesting activity and determines the best method of acquisition as well as the most appropriate contract type to satisfy the government's needs. During this initial stage the CO will validate the organization's requirements, ensuring that the intended use of commercial augmentation is in compliance with the FAR and in the best interests of the government.

5. After the CO determines the feasibility of the requirement, he or she will begin the solicitation process by establishing contract terms and conditions.

6. The CO, in consultation with other technical experts, conducts market research to determine which vendors are capable of providing the services. During this process the CO evaluates past performance of vendors to determine which companies have the experience and capabilities to adequately satisfy the requirement. The CO will also conduct a cost analysis to ensure that prices paid for services or products are fair and reasonable.

7. The CO will appoint a contracting officer's representative (COR) to provide technical assistance. The COR or contracting officer's technical representative (COTR) will act on behalf of the CO for certain oversight and surveillance functions and assist with other aspects of contract development and administration. This appointment must be made in writing.

8. The CO issues a solicitation in order to receive proposals from likely vendors and then manages the selection process.

9. Once the CO receives bids from potential vendors, he or she conducts the competition to select the best vendor and then conducts negotiations on behalf of the government.

10. Once the contract is signed, the CO takes responsibility for administering the execution until termination. This process includes overseeing all administrative actions necessary to ensuring satisfactory performance. The CO bears responsibility for safeguarding the government's interest against undue risks, liabilities, or unsatisfactory performance by the vendor.

11. Once the CO signs the contract, he or she is the only approval authority for changes, modifications, extensions, or termination. The contracting officer has sole authority to cancel a bid and modify or terminate the contract based on changing government requirements. As a rule, contract modifications must be made formally in writing and cannot go beyond the general scope of the agreement.
12. The CO will make all final determinations with regard to disputes over contractor performance, protests, or claims on behalf of the government or the vendor.
13. The CO is responsible for ensuring that funds are available when the government makes an obligation to a vendor. The CO coordinates with the organizational financial officer to validate and authorize payments to the vendor.
14. In cooperation with the COR and government supervisor, the CO maintains constant cognizance of contract performance and ensures that all administrative and performance information is adequately documented and maintained in the official contract files.
15. The CO is responsible for closing out or terminating the contract at the end of the period of performance.

The Role of the Contracting Officer's Representative (COR)

The contracting officer's representative (COR) is the individual designated by the contracting officer to act as his or her representative assisting in administering the contract. The COR accomplishes these tasks by verifying contractor performance, inspecting work, and maintaining liaison and communication between the government supervisor, contracting officer, and vendor. The COR ensures that all contracted services are delivered to the government according to requirements specified in the contract language. The source of the COR's authority is a written letter of designation from the CO.

There is no specific statutory requirement in the FAR mandating the training requirements or qualifications for the COR. The rules and requirements below generally apply for most organizations, but it is important to remember that each government department or agency may establish internal standards, requirements, and qualifications for contracting officer's representatives. Generally speaking, all CORs should be trained in basic contract management and administration functions. Below are some general standards and expectations that should apply to all appointed CORs.

Basic Requirements for Contracting Officer's Representatives

- The COR must be a government employee, unless otherwise authorized by agency or organizational regulation.

- The COR must be qualified by training and experience commensurate with the responsibilities to be delegated in accordance with agency or organizational regulations.
- COR functions may not be delegated or changed, except by written order of the appointing CO.
- The COR does not have the authority to make any commitments or changes that effect price, quality, quantity, delivery, or other terms and conditions of the contract.
- COR appointment must be designated in writing and furnished to the contractor and contract-administration office. The designation letter should, at a minimum, identify the limitations on the COR's authority and the period covered by the designation.
- The COR must maintain a file for each contract assigned. At a minimum, this file must include a copy of the contracting officer's letter of designation, appropriate documentation describing the COR's duties and responsibilities, and a record of all actions taken in accordance with the delegation of authority.

Supervisor's Interactions with the Contracting Officer's Representative

In all cases, the contracting officer's representative should be the supervisor's first point of contact for any questions concerning the performance of contractors in the government workplace. A good relationship between the government supervisor and the COR is arguably the most important element for ensuring the successful outcome of a government-contractor partnership. The COR is the supervisor's primary point of contact for resolving any disputes or correcting performance issues with the contractor workforce.

It is critical that the supervisor and COR maintain effective and frequent communication to ensure that the government's needs are met and the terms of the contract fully satisfied. Due to the importance of this relationship, it is necessary for the government supervisor to fully understand the COR's roles, responsibilities, authorities, and limitations. This knowledge will enable the government supervisor to understand the COR's role and help develop a cooperative and productive relationship.

First and foremost, it is important to remember that the COR's authorization and power is not the same as the CO's. The COR does not have the authority to enter into a contract on behalf of the government or to modify the terms of an existing contract. Furthermore, the CO cannot delegate authority to the COR to make any commitments or changes that affect price, quality, quantity, delivery, or other terms and conditions of the contract. The best way to understand the duties and responsibilities of the COR is to equate him or her to the eyes and ears of the CO. Since the CO is frequently far removed from the actual site of contract performance, the COR's job is to monitor the contract and maintain record of the contractor's performance. The COR is designated by the CO to perform inspections of the contractor's work and approve the government's acceptance of products or services.

Typically the contracting officer will appoint a single COR for a particular contract, but this may vary depending on the specific circumstances of the contract and the unique requirements for surveillance. The COR must be a government employee and must be qualified by training and experience in accordance with the internal polices and regulations of the agency or organization. The CO may also appoint additional technical monitors (sometimes referred to as contracting officer's technical representatives, or COTRs) to monitor other aspects of the contractor's work.

The COR's role may encompass a wide range of duties and activities throughout all phases of the acquisition process, including consultation during the pre-award process, administrative functions, monitoring performance, and dealing with contract termination. Ideally, the COR will be appointed early on in the requirements-development process and will remain closely involved throughout the administration and closeout procedures to ensure continuity and effective surveillance during the life of the contract.

Because of the COR's central role in administering the contract and conducting surveillance activities, it is critically important that the workplace supervisor fully understand their duties and responsibilities. The COR is the supervisor's primary interface for all questions and issues concerning management and oversight of the contractor workforce. The list below provides a general overview of the expected duties, responsibilities, and authorities of the COR.

Duties of the Contracting Officer's Representative

1. The COR's primary function is to work with the contracting officer to provide oversight and ensure that the vendor delivers all products and services in accordance with the specifications outlined in the contract. The COR is expected to maintain direct and frequent communication with both the vendor and the CO in order to ensure satisfactory performance.
2. The COR is appointed in writing by the contracting officer. The appointment memorandum should clearly describe the expectations for performance and limits of the COR's authorities. Appointment should not be made until the COR has received all training required by agency or organizational policy. The COR is required to acknowledge in writing the receipt of the contracting officer's letter of delegation. Authorities delegated to the COR by the contracting officer cannot be redelegated without the express approval of the CO.

3. The appointment memorandum from the contracting officer will outline the extent of the COR's authority to act on behalf of the CO and will provide any specified limitations to their authority. It is important to remember that, while the COR acts on behalf of the CO, he or she does not have the authority to make any commitments to a vendor that affect the price, quality, quantity, product delivery, statement of work, delivery schedule, period of performance, administrative provisions, or other terms and conditions of the contract. If the COR crosses these boundaries or exceeds the strict description of their delegated authorities, they run the risk of making an unauthorized commitment on behalf of the government.

4. In certain situations the COR may task other individuals with assisting with monitoring functions and other administrative requirements, particularly when the COR is not physically colocated at the site of the contractor's performance or when work is being performed at multiple remote locations. In such situations the COR should receive prior approval from the CO and ensure that all individuals with delegated responsibilities possess necessary knowledge, experience, and guidance to perform their duties.

5. During the initial contract-development phase, the COR may assist the CO in a variety of ways, including analysis of technical requirements for products or services, assistance with market research, contract development, solicitation procedures, managing the competition process, preparation of statement of work or statement of objectives, source selection, and any other duties as required by the contracting officer.

6. During the contract-administration process the COR will serve as the primary technical representative. The COR will typically represent the CO in all technical meetings with the program manager, government supervisor, and vendor. They will assist the parties in understanding the technical requirements of the agreement and resolving disputes in interpretation of the contract.

7. The COR will frequently assist in developing the contract-surveillance plan, monitoring procedures, and performance metrics used to assess the vendor's performance. The COR will serve as the contract's primary technical monitor, confirming delivery of all goods and services and ensuring that work is completed in accordance with the contract requirements and quality control standards.

8. The COR, with the contracting officer, is responsible for ensuring that the government satisfies all contractual commitments to the vendor. This may include providing access to facilities, equipment, or training, as stipulated in the contract, required for the vendor to complete their work.

9. The COR has the primary responsibility for implementing and monitoring the quality-assurance-surveillance plan, describing the standards, schedule, and procedures for inspecting the contractor's performance. This plan should clearly define the standards of delivery and thresholds for acceptable and unacceptable performance.

10. The COR will serve as the subject matter expert for government supervisors relating to contract performance, administrative matters, best practices, or any other concerns relating to the operation of the government-contractor workforce.

11. The COR will provide technical interpretations and clarifications on the terms of the contract for both the vendor and the government supervisor.

12. The COR will monitor certain human resources functions in coordination with the vendor. This may include, but is not limited to, compliance with applicable contract laws, job safety requirements, observed violations of labor standards, monitoring contractor time worked, inspecting contractor record-keeping procedures, and ensuring enforcement of all health and safety requirements. Additionally, the COR will ensure that the vendor appropriately assigns contractor employees with the required capabilities, qualifications, and experience in accordance with the contract statement of work.

13. The COR will document any requested modification to contract language and provide this information to the contracting office. Neither the supervisor nor the COR can direct the contractor to modify any aspect of their tasks, delivery schedule, or standard of work until the contracting officer has authorized and approved the modification.

14. It is the duty of the COR to provide written notification to the contracting officer when a vendor demonstrates reoccurring deficiencies in performance or failure to satisfy scheduled delivery standards. The COR is expected to notify the CO in writing of any unsatisfactory performance or deficiencies in contractor performance and to provide a recommendation for remedial action. When deficiencies are noted, it is the responsibility of the COR to verify that the contractor has taken remedial actions and corrected identified problems.

15. The COR is responsible for coordinating any specialized technical inspections or quality-assurance evaluations necessary to monitoring the delivery of goods or services in accordance with the standards established by the contract.

16. The COR will verify that the contractor has performed all required internal technical inspections and quality control measures in accordance with contract specifications.

17. In cooperation with the organizational security officer and government supervisor, the COR will ensure that all of the vendors employees have appropriate clearances required for work on government facilities and automation systems and for network access.
18. The COR supervises the contractor's management and accountability of government-furnished property. In the absence of a designated property manager, the COR is responsible for ensuring property accountability, maintenance, and storage of government tools, supplies, equipment, and systems used by contractor employees in the execution of their tasks. The COR protects the government's interest in management of all government property and equipment used by the contractor
19. The COR will ensure that the contractor has access to all government regulations, technical publications, manuals, policy letters, and written guidance required to perform their tasks.
20. The COR executes the performance-assessment plan developed by the requiring element to ensure that the contractor is performing their duties in accordance with the standards outlined in the contract.
21. The COR is responsible for maintaining records of all contractor performance documentation, inspection results, memorandums for record (MFR), official correspondence from the vendor, and other records relating to contractor performance and necessary for closeout of the contract.
22. The COR will assist the supervisor in monitoring for any potential ethical or legal violations in the workplace. This includes reporting conflict-of-interest violations or instances of contractor misconduct or fraud, waste, and abuse.
23. The COR is expected to offer the CO recommendations on contract modifications and termination actions. These recommendations should be made in consultation with the government supervisor in situations where the government's operations will be significantly affected by the action.
24. The COR will help prepare and document the contractor's past-performance assessment.
25. The COR will assist the CO in contract closeout or termination procedures as requested.
26. It is also important for government supervisors to recognize several things that the COR cannot or should not do, such as

- awarding, signing, or modifying a contract
- obligating government funds

- granting exceptions or deviations from the standards established by the contract (referred to as *constructive changes*)
- requesting that vendors perform tasks or services not stipulated in the contract
- making changes in the contract that affect price, quantity, quality, and delivery
- expanding the scope of the contract activities or authorizing additional man-hours, overtime, or payments
- authorizing the vendor's use or purchase of government property or services not stipulated in the contract
- changing or extending the period of performance

The Role of the Vendor Program Manager

The vendor's program manager, or site lead, directs, supervises, and manages the work of the company's employees at the site of performance. He or she is ultimately responsible for ensuring that the quality of work for their employees is in accordance with the set standards of the contract. In many cases the site lead will work very closely with the government supervisor in managing the daily operations of the hybrid workforce.

While the COR is the government supervisor's primary interface for dealing with issues of contractor performance, the relationship with the vendor's site manager is nearly as important. Due to proximity and the frequency of interaction with the vendor's manager, it is important that the government supervisor understand the expectations for this relationship and what role this individual plays in the execution of the contract.

During day-to-day operations, the government supervisor's efforts should be primarily focused on managing activities of government employees. Interface with the vendor's site manager will typically involve issues such as workflow management and communication of requirements to the vendor's workforce. Generally speaking, the supervisor should not address specific concerns with performance matters directly to the vendor's site manager. Observed discrepancies or shortfalls in the contractor's performance should be reported through an established and formalized mechanism directly to the COR. It is then the COR's responsibility to resolve these issues in consultation with the CO and vendor's manager. The reasoning behind this approach is not to create an additional layer of unnecessary bureaucracy between the supervisor and vendor's site manager and contractor workforce but rather to protect the government's interests by ensuring that the supervisor does not overstep his or her authority by directing the contractor's work. This approach also preserves the integrity of the surveillance plan by ensuring that the COR is informed and aware of all issues concerning the contractor's performance.

In cases where a supervisor deals directly with the vendor's site manager to resolve performance issues, there are several potential risks. The first concern is the potential for personal-services violations if the vendor's manager or employees habitually receive substantive direction and guidance directly from the government supervisor. This type of directive engagement subverts the proper role of the COR and contracting officer as responsible agents for surveillance and evaluation of the vendor's performance. Furthermore, when a supervisor provides directive corrections, work modifications, or other substantive instructions to the site manager, there is a risk that the terms of the contract could be misinterpreted in the process. This could result in a potential scope-of-work violation or unauthorized obligation if the vendor's employees are directed to modify work or perform duties falling outside the terms of the contract. Thus, the necessity for supervisors to use the COR as the mechanism for resolving performance deficiencies, rather than dealing directly with the vendor's manager, protects both the government and the integrity of the contractual relationship.

While the terms of the supervisor–site manager relationship may seem excessively narrow and restrictive, it is important to remember that each workplace is unique. There is no fixed protocol or methodology for how this relationship should work. Every organization will have its own dynamics and internal operating procedures based on the nature of the requirement and characteristics of the workforce. The doctrinal expectation that the supervisor always communicate directly with the COR should not discourage or inhibit a supervisor's close and effective partnership with the vendor's site manager.

There is no precise line designating what issues must be resolved between the supervisor and the site manager and what must be resolved by the COR. Building a positive working relationship will enable many minor workplace concerns and technical challenges to be resolved without going to the COR for every single matter requiring clarification. In defining this line, government supervisors must apply a certain degree of common sense and professional discretion. Certainly any issues involving habitual performance deficiencies by the contractor, questions involving the scope of allowable work, or matters of ethical or legal concern must be immediately brought to the attention of the COR. Yet, even in these areas there is some ambiguity in expectations.

Certainly there is great inefficiency involved in requiring the COR to become involved with every single minor technical question that arises during the course of daily operations. This is particularly true in cases when the COR may not be colocated at the site of performance. In such situations the supervisor must apply good judgment in managing his or her relationship with the vendor's manager in order to accomplish the required tasks. Open communication between the supervisor and the site manager, as well as a common understanding of goals, will go a long way toward ensuring a successful partnership while maintaining the integrity of the government-contractor relationship.

In order to ensure the proper function of the blended workplace, it is important for the supervisor to understand the proper role of the vendor's site manager and their responsibilities in the workplace. The list below provides some general guidelines and explanations as to what the supervisor should expect from the vendor's site manager. Beyond this, much of what occurs on a day-to-day basis in the workplace depends less on specific rules and regulations and more on the quality of communication and cooperation between the supervisor and the site manager.

Roles and Responsibilities of the Vendor's Site Manager

1. The vendor's site manager directs, supervises, and controls the work of the company's employees. They are responsible for ensuring the quality of their employees' work in accordance with the terms of the contract.
2. The site manager should be familiar with the terms of the contract. He or she should clearly understand the expectations and requirements outlined in the statement of work and how their employees' services support the government's process.
3. Site managers should be technical experts in the particular work of their employees and have excellent understanding of the goods or services provided to the government. Additionally, the site manager should understand the overall goals of the contract, the workflow process, and how tasks are assigned from the government. This will enable the site manager to properly organize the team to best accomplish the required tasks.
4. The site manager is the vendor's the primary interface with the contracting officer's representative for resolution of performance issues.
5. It is primarily the responsibility of the site manager to ensure that the contract standards of quality and schedule of delivery are satisfied. Some contracts will also stipulate that the contractor develop and implement a quality control plan (QCP) to monitor the products or services produced by their team. The site manager is expected to work with the COR to determine the methodology for documenting and reporting this information.
6. The site manager will handle all administrative and personnel matters pertaining to the vendor's workforce, such as leave, sick days, time cards, promotions, evaluations, disciplinary actions, and compensation determinations.

7. The site manager and vendor are responsible for ensuring that their employees are properly trained and prepared for all duties and tasks required by the contract. In some cases, due to unplanned contingencies such as policy changes, procedural modifications, or the introduction of new technology, the entire government-contractor workforce may require additional training not specifically stipulated in the contract. If the government determines that there is a benefit to including the contractor workforce in the training, this may be coordinated between the vendor, COR, and contracting officer. In most other cases the contractor is responsible for providing whatever training is required for their employees in order to satisfy tasks stipulated in the statement of work.

8. The site manager is primarily responsible for taking remedial actions to resolve discrepancies or problems with the delivery of goods or with service failing to satisfy the government's quality standards.

9. As a general rule, the vendor, through the site manager, will be responsible for providing all equipment, supplies, and materials for their employees. The exceptions to this general rule are for items specifically identified as government-provided material in the contract.

10. The site manager will initiate administrative or disciplinary actions for individual contractor employees who violate applicable government rules, contract requirements, or regulations of the workplace. Disciplinary actions are not the responsibility of the government supervisor unless a situation requires immediate intervention by a government employee for reasons of safety or security.

11. The vendor and site manager will administer all internal company policies for awards, compensation, incentives, and bonus programs for their employees. The supervisor should play no role with internal company compensation decisions.

12. The site manager bears primary responsibility for the safety and security of their employees in the workplace. The government supervisor should work with the site manager to ensure that sufficient training materials are provided to the company so their employees are aware of all applicable safety and security policies if work is performed at a government facility.

13. The vendor, with input from the site manager, is responsible for selecting employees who will best fulfill the terms, conditions, and requirements of the contract. Depending on the stipulations of the contract, there may be a requirement for the vendor to provide résumés or background information for government review prior to assigning particular individuals, but this is not always the case. The site manager is not prohibited from soliciting general advice from the government

supervisor about appropriate skills and qualifications necessary for sat-isfying a particular government requirement, but the supervisor must avoid giving the impression that he or she is directing the hiring or assignment process of company employees. The supervisor should not request to review the résumés of potential company hires or individu-als assigned to the team unless specifically authorized by the terms of the contract or approved by the COR.

14. It is important to remember that ultimately the success or failure of the government-contractor relationship depends on a collaborative effort. It is both appropriate and helpful for government supervisors to ask site managers and contractor employees for advice and recom-mendations on how to improve the government's process and output. Government supervisors should make every effort to leverage the knowledge, experience, and resources of the contractor team in order to enhance the performance and efficiency of their organization. The site manager should be welcomed to provide input and recommen-dations on how to improve the government's process efficiency and quality of output.

15. In addition to being aware of what the site manager should be doing, it is also important to be aware of some specific things they should not be doing. A few basic tips are provided below.

- Site managers and their employees will not direct, task, or control government personnel.
- They will not participate in functions relating to the administration of the contract or other procurement-related activities.
- They cannot supervise or direct the employees of other vendors.
- They will not knowingly perform inherently governmental functions or tasks clearly out of the contract's scope of work.
- They will not independently interpret major terms or aspects of the contract without consulting with the COR and contracting officer for clarification.

The Role of the Government Supervisor

To provide effective management of a blended government-contractor work-force it is important that supervisors clearly understand their roles, as well as the limitations of their authority in dealing with contractor employees. This means clearly identifying the "lanes in the road," so to speak, in order to avoid overstepping boundaries in the workplace. There is no specific formula that applies to every workforce or every government contract. Each blended team will have unique challenges based on the function of the organization, differing operational requirements, and the nature of the contracts themselves. Given such varied circumstances it is difficult to provide a specific set of rules for every possible situation. Therefore, the tips below are generic in nature, intended to apply to the broad range of circumstances and challenges of most blended workforces. Keeping in mind these general rules of thumb will help ensure that the blended team best meets the government's needs and operates in an efficient, legal, and ethical manner.

What Government Supervisors Should Do

1. Communicate often and effectively with the COR
2. Be familiar with the contract, understand the statement of work, and know the standards of delivery for products and services
3. Be familiar with the roles and responsibilities of all the players, including both the government-acquisition team and the vendor's management team
4. Carefully document any and all observations concerning contractor performance, providing this feedback directly to the contracting officer's representative
5. Conduct a detailed operational analysis of the organization to determine the optimal utilization of contractor support and work with the vendor's program manager to ensure that their resources are being used in the most efficient manner
6. Organize the government-contractor workforce in order to leverage the unique skills and experience of all employees and consider how government-contractor teams will be formed and the appropriate level of government supervision and oversight required for their tasks
7. Ensure that all directive instructions, substantive changes, and assignment of tasking to the contractor workforce are communicated through the vendor's site manager and manage the overall process of the workplace while allowing the vendor to manage people and tasks
8. Make the vendor a partner in seeking better techniques and solutions for government operations and seek advice and assistance from the vendor's site manager on process improvements and management decisions that will best employ and leverage the skills and labor of the contractor workforce
9. Ensure that every task and requirement assigned to the contractor workforce is linked to a delivery schedule and objective standards of quality
10. Develop a workflow process that applies statistical measures to evaluate the efficiency and productivity of the contractor workforce

11. Seek dynamic equilibrium in workflow management, making, to the greatest extent possible, the assignment of tasks and project requirements to the contractor workforce controlled and predictable and avoiding lags or surges in requirements that will alternately underutilize or overwhelm the contractor workforce, and seeking efficiency in the government's process so that the vendor can effectively task his or her employees
12. Play a cooperative role with the COR developing performance measures to evaluate the contractor performance, providing metrics for quantifying the quality and efficiency of the contractor's output
13. Work closely with the COR to gather performance data and feedback, facilitating inspections, conducting quality control reviews and performance evaluations of the contractors work
14. Continuously analyze the government's requirements as operations evolve, being prepared to collaborate with the contracting officer and acquisition team to request modifications to the contract when necessary
15. Educate the COR and the contracting officer on the organization's internal processes, requirements and challenges, keeping them informed on how the contractor workforce can better contribute to the organization's process and productivity and making the CO and COR partners in daily operations
16. Train the government workforce on proper government-contractor relations, including education on the appropriate procedures for dealing with contractor employees, legal and ethical considerations, the chain of authority for contractor personnel, and how tasks and requirements should be assigned to the contractor workforce
17. Always inform the COR immediately in the case of any potential conflict of interest, security violation, or legal or ethical concerns with the contractor workforce

What Government Supervisors Should Not Do

1. Do not direct, manage, or modify the work of contract employees. Do not become involved with or interfere in the site manager's supervision of their employees, unless it is to stop a direct violation of the organization's regulations, security procedures, or safety requirements.
2. Do not request delivery of any task, service, or product not clearly stipulated in the contract language.
3. Do not request an individual contractor or vendor to undertake new tasks or assignments outside the scope of work.

4. Do not authorize an extension of work beyond the stated period of the contract. This includes issuing any instructions for the contractor to start or stop work. This can only be done by the contracting officer or the COR under direction from the CO.
5. Do not offer independent interpretation or clarification of the contract language, scope of work, or tasks performed by the contractor. These functions are the responsibility of the COR and contracting officer.
6. Do not enter into any agreement or negotiation for a vendor's services. Do not authorize any promises of work or obligation on behalf of the government without going through the COR and contracting officer.
7. Do not approve or disapprove a vendor's personnel-management decisions. This includes authorizing personnel actions, approving vacation time or sick days, hiring or termination actions, overseeing disciplinary proceedings, conducting performance reviews, approving promotions or position changes, offering incentives, or making bonus determinations.
8. Do not approve expenditure of government funds to the contractor or vendor. Be aware that government personnel may become liable for any commitment or obligation, even those inadvertently communicated to a contractor employee or vendor.
9. Do not enter into any discussions with the vendor or contractor employees concerning future contract awards, options, extensions, budgeting information relating to commitments on contracts, speculation on the terms or conditions of renewals, rebids, or new contract proposals.

4

Understanding the Government-Contractor Relationship and the Supervisor's Role in the Contract Administration Process

Understanding the Government-Contractor Relationship

GOVERNMENT AND CONTRACTOR EMPLOYEES frequently work side-by-side, often with little distinction in the nature and conditions of work they perform, yet there are critical distinctions between them that must be recognized and respected. It is the supervisor's responsibility to ensure that these workplace boundaries are clearly defined and that all employees abide by these distinctions. Supervisors must continually reinforce the fact that contractor employees have entitlements, duties, and expectations distinct from those of government employees. These differences extend to virtually every aspect of employment, including matters of compensation, legal liabilities, hiring and termination actions, promotion, education and training opportunities, use of government equipment and facilities, regulatory requirements, and ethics rules in the workplace.

It is also important to remember that government employees and contract workers have fundamentally different obligations. The duty of government employees is to their department or agency, and ultimately to act in the best interests of the taxpayers. Conversely, the contractor's obligations are to their company and the interests of its shareholders. The most fundamental distinction between a government and a contractor employee may be summed up as public purpose versus private profit.

Government employees are managed by civil service rules established by the Office of Personnel Management. As such, they are subject to a variety of regulations, laws, agency rules, ethical standards, and commonly accepted codes of conduct applicable to all federal employees. Conversely, contractors are governed primarily by the terms of their contract and respective company policy. In some cases they may also be subject to specific governmental regulations explicitly stated in the contract as well as to certain mandated health and safety regulations applicable to government facilities where they may perform work. In some cases, depending on the nature of the contract, there may be additional security requirements that apply to all personnel working on particular projects. These types of requirements should be clearly stipulated in the contract.

While government supervisors should encourage workforce integration and team building, they must do so in a manner that recognizes the distinctions between employees. Supervisors must use precise language when addressing issues such as entitlements and responsibilities, remembering that government-contractor teams are blended only in that they should provide seamless support toward accomplishment of the contract objectives. In most other ways the workforce is in fact not blended, particularly in terms of management structure, entitlements, duties, expectations, and responsibilities. Effective supervision of the hybrid team requires recognition and enforcement of these distinctions in order to maintain the integrity of the government-contractor relationship.

One of the most important reasons to maintain strict distinctions between government and contractor employees is in order to avoid potential problems with personal-services violations. The FAR defines personal services as those contracts "characterized by the employer-employee relationship they create between the government and the contractor personnel." Generally speaking, agencies of the federal government are not permitted to award personal-services contracts unless specifically authorized by statute or special exemption. The FAR states that an employer-employee relationship exists when the terms of the contract or manner of its administration requires relatively continuous supervision and control of the contractor employee by a government employee or supervisor.[1]

Ultimately it is the responsibility of the contracting officer to ensure that the contract statement of work or performance work statement does not contain tasks or requirements that would create personal-services violations. The COR should reinforce these measures by providing effective oversight of daily operations, good contract administration, and appropriate training to supervisors and government employees working with the contractor team. Though ideally these measures provide adequate protection ensuring that personal-services violations do not inadvertently occur, there are many instances where contracting officers and even CORs are not present at the site of performance or have infrequent interaction with the government supervisor. This is an unfortunate reality of many service contracts, a situation made worse by significant shortfalls of trained contract-administration personnel.

Given this situation, it is incumbent upon the supervisor to take significant responsibly for ensuring that good administrative practices are followed in their workplace. In many cases the CO and the COR will simply not have the time, proximity, or awareness of the day-to-day management issues to effectively serve as agents of oversight. This is not how it should be, but this situation reflects the current reality for many government-service contracts. In such cases the supervisor becomes the responsible authority for ensuring that contracted support is legal and appropriately utilized. Thus, it is critical that the supervisor create a workplace environment that reinforces the distinctions between government and contractor employees.

Adhering to some basic rules of thumb will help to avoid most situations in which personal-services violations are likely to occur and to reduce the chances of other inappropriate management practices concerning contractor personnel. Supervisors should keep the following tips in mind.

- Contractors must always be clearly identified in the workplace so that there is no confusion as to the nature of their status.
- Contractors should only perform work based on the terms of the written contract and statement of work.
- Supervisors and government employees must recognize the legal chain of authority over contractor employees. Contractors receive instructions and orders from their designated company supervisor and not from government employees. This includes workplace guidance, task clarifications, changes to requirements or the performance of duties, and modifications to standards of performance or processes.
- Contractor personnel cannot be placed in a position where they are under supervision, direction, or evaluation of a government employee.
- Contractor personnel should not be placed in positions of command, supervision, administration, or control over government personnel or the contractors of other vendors.
- Contractor personnel should not be listed on government organizational charts or rosters.
- Contractors should not be used for direction and administration of government procurement activities.
- Government supervisors must not take any action toward the contractor that suggests the existence of an employer-employee relationship. This includes activities such as directly supervising contractor employees; stipulating duty hours; keeping personnel records; approving time cards, vacation, or sick days; maintaining personnel records; approving bonuses; or developing duty rosters.

The Basics of Contract Administration

Contract administration is a broad term describing the practices and techniques for initiating acquisitions, developing and implementing contract agreements, monitoring and evaluating performance, and conducting final closeout of contracts. Basically it encompasses all of the steps required for managing the entire lifecycle of the agreement.

The primary purpose of the contract-administration process is to ensure that the government receives the goods or services that it has paid for and that delivery is accomplished according to the standards outlined in the agreement. This means ensuring that all deliverables are provided on time, within budget, and to the quality standards described in the contract. The exact process of administration will vary significantly from contract to contract depending on the type of agreement and nature of the goods or services being provided.

The administration process is primarily the responsibility of the contracting officer and the COR, but often there will be other players involved, including technical experts, auditors, accountants, lawyers, and other procurement specialists. Generally speaking, government supervisors will only be exposed to relatively limited aspects of the overall administrative process. But in some cases supervisors and government employees will play an important supporting role in facilitating the administration process. For this reason it is important for government supervisors and employees to have some understanding of the steps in the process and best practices for effective execution.

As has been previously discussed, effective contract administration starts with developing a clear statement of the work describing the tasks that the contractor will perform. Without this fundamental element, it is virtually impossible to effectively administer a contract and monitor the quality of performance. A well-written statement of work or performance objectives are critically important, since they form the basis on which to evaluate the contractor's performance and to determine if the government has received fair value for the taxpayers' money.

The Supervisor's Role in Contract Administration

Although the contracting officer and COR are ultimately responsible for overseeing the administration of the contract, the supervisor and entire government workforce play an important part in the success of the government-contractor partnership. Even the best-written contract will only be as good as the quality of their administration and oversight. If the acquisition team fails to plan for effective administration, it is unlikely that the government will receive a desirable outcome for the taxpayer. Since the contracting officer and COR may not always be present at the site of performance or have insight into every aspect of the contractor's daily operations, it is imperative that the government supervisor play a proactive role, assisting the COR in administrative and monitoring tasks whenever possible.

In some contracts there will be instances in which the government supervisor plays a more significant cooperative role in development, administration, and oversight of the contract. The best contracts are generally those in which the acquisition team solicits input from a variety of subject matter experts to quantify the government's requirements and establish favorable conditions for a successful partnership. The contracting officer and COR are acquisition professionals, but they may lack extensive experience in the particular field or process that the contractor is supporting. For this reason, the acquisition team will rely on the supervisor for advice and guidance on developing and implementing an effective plan for monitoring and evaluating contractor performance.

Knowledge about the details of the contract, performance requirements, and delivery standards should not simply be the purview of the contracting officer, COR, and acquisition team. There is enormous benefit in the entire government team, including supervisors and employees, being familiar with all aspects of the contract and the expectations for vendor performance. Supervisors should ensure all assigned government employees are familiar with the basic terms of the contract. Too often, this is an afterthought in the workplace. Supervisors and government employees think, "That stuff is the COR's business, not mine." But particularly with PBSA methodology, the success or failure of the program depends on a team approach whereby all members take responsibly for ensuring that the contractor delivers the required product or service to standard. Knowledge of the contract language and terms will better enable both supervisors and employees to monitor progress, provide constructive support to the contractor, and to ensure that delivery standards are met and that all work is conducted in a safe, legal, and ethical manner.

Basic Rules of Thumb for Effective Administration of Service-Based Contracts

The Office of Federal Procurement Policy offers some basic guidelines for ensuring that government contracts are properly administered. It is helpful for supervisors to keep these in mind as they consider their contribution to the development and administration of the contract.

- Contract language accurately describes the government's need, the tasks performed, or the problem to be resolved by the vendor's service.

- Services are used in such a way that ensures the government retains inherently governmental decision-making authority.
- Services are obtained in the most cost-effective manner, using full and open competition, and are free from potential conflicts of interest.
- Responsible government personnel are adequately trained and experienced to manage and oversee all aspects of the contract-administration functions.
- Effective management practices are in place to prevent waste, fraud, and abuse and to ensure that the government receives value from the contractor.

Supervisor's Tips for Facilitating Effective Contract Administration

As the acquisition team begins preparation of requirements statements and develops performance criteria and evaluation methodologies, they may call on government supervisors to provide input based on their specialized knowledge of the work process.

Below are a few critical areas in which a government supervisor may provide support to the acquisition team so as to strengthen the overall acquisition and contract-administration process.

Assisting in the Acquisition-Planning Process

During the initial planning phase it is critical that the entire acquisition team have a clear understanding of the government's requirements. The most important step is determining exactly what it is that the government wants from the vendor and providing clear and detailed guidance in the request for proposal. In the preacquisition phase the government supervisor may provide specialized technical knowledge of the government's processes and description of the requirements that the contractor will be asked to support.

Supervisors can offer important contributions to the work of the acquisition team by providing detailed specifications of the required services, delivery standards, production schedules, prerequisite skills, and necessary qualifications of the contractor workforce. The success of the partnership will be largely determined during this initial phase as the requirements language is developed. Inaccurate or vague requirement statements inevitably result in poorly written contracts that do not inform potential vendors of the government's actual needs or that provide insufficient guidance for the contractor to develop accurate cost estimates, performance plans, or select the best personnel to perform the task.

Supervisors may also play an important role when existing contracts are up for extension or rebid. At this juncture they can work with the contracting officer and COR to develop any modifications to existing requirement statements based on their knowledge of the government's changing operational demands.

Defining Contractor Roles and Responsibilities in the Workplace

Due to their familiarity with day-to-day operations and requirements of the government workplace, supervisors possess very detailed knowledge about the nature of the contractors' role and how they will best contribute to the accomplishment of a project or process. As the acquisition team develops the statement of work and outlines the project requirements, the supervisor's input will be extremely valuable, providing context on the contractor's work requirements and special considerations for performance. This may include input on such matters as specific regulatory guidance, performance conditions, and technical standards that must be included in the contract language. These inputs will help define the contractor's scope of work and articulate their contribution to the government's overall process. The supervisor will also be able to provide detailed information concerning the actual function of the workplace, such as the types of technology, equipment, or facilities that the government must furnish to the contractor to enable them to perform their work.

Developing Performance Standards and a Delivery Schedule

The supervisor can provide important information concerning details of the workflow process, such as how requirements are tasked to the workforce, project milestones, delivery schedules, and required performance standards. This input is particularly important in the case of service-based contracts. While contracts for goods are typically very detailed in their technical specifications and apply equivalent commercial-production standards, service-based contracts are sometimes vague in articulating precise standards of delivery. It is often difficult to define performance standards for services, particularly when the product to be delivered by the contractor is conceptual in nature, such as analysis, process development, report writing, or administrative or staff-support functions. This challenge is made more difficult when the tasks or requirements do not have directly comparable commercial standards for performance. In these cases it is even more important that experienced government supervisors contribute to contract development and lend their expert knowledge of the workflow process so that the contractor's contribution can be defined, quantified, and measured.

Establishing Efficient Government-Workflow Processes

Perhaps the supervisor's most important function in facilitating effective contract administration is developing and implementing a workflow process and operational environment enabling the contractor to deliver their services without disruption due to inefficiencies in the government's process. The contractor may bring all the appropriate skills and expertise to the job, but if the government fails to provide a system to effectively task and manage the flow of work to the contractor, the partnership will ultimately be unsuccessful.

As a general rule, government supervisors should design process systems that minimize the need for continual government supervision of the contractor's day-to-day activities. A workflow process should be developed that reduces direct involvement of government employees in the tasking, assigning, and daily supervision of contractor work. These functions should be primarily the responsibility of the vendor's site manager. Supervisors should focus their efforts on managing overall process efficiency and directing the government's portion of workforce operations.

Supervisors can also optimize the utility of the contractor workforce by designing systems that minimize surges and lulls in workflow. It is particularly important to avoid situations where the contractor workforce is either overwhelmed with requirements or underutilized for periods of time. A well-designed and predictable workflow system will bring greater efficiency to the process and maximize contractor performance by permitting the site manager to better plan and program the work of their employees.

Developing Effective Surveillance Plans

After defining the requirements and developing an efficient workflow system, the next critical step for the supervisor is assisting the COR and contracting officer with implementing an effective contract-surveillance plan.

The contractor's delivery of goods and services will be only as good as the process used to monitor and enforce standards established by the contract. In this process the supervisor can serve two important functions: first, offering their technical expertise to the contracting officer in developing standards and methodologies for measuring contractor performance and, second, assisting the COR in implementing an effective surveillance plan in the workplace.

Since the supervisor will have the most detailed knowledge of the workplace processes, his or her expertise and input is vital for developing an effective surveillance plan to monitor the contractor's work. The CO and COR will rely on supervisors, project managers, and technical experts to clearly define performance standards, contractor workload estimates, inspection schedules, monitoring techniques, surveillance methodologies, and quality control checklists. The supervisor may also provide applicable references—policies, regulations, or product examples that will help to better define the quality standards expected of the contractor. These contributions will greatly assist the CO and COR as they integrate these requirements and standards into the contract language.

Supervisors may also assist the acquisition team by providing a recommendation as to the number of government personnel that are needed to adequately conduct surveillance and oversight functions. Depending on the complexity of the operation, this may require the appointment of additional technical monitors. The supervisor and acquisition team must ensure that there is an appropriate ratio of government personnel to contractors to ensure adequate monitoring of their functions. Supervisors can also provide input and guidance to the CO and COR concerning any unique requirements for the technical monitors, such as specialized training and procedures for conducting routine inspections and evaluations.

In some circumstances the COR may not have the opportunity for daily, direct observation of a contractor's performance. This is particularly true if the contractor performs work in multiple locations, deployed environments, or remote sites. In such circumstances the government supervisor plays a critical role in facilitating the surveillance plan and providing the COR with performance data and feedback so that they may properly assess the vendor's work against the stated requirements of the contract.

While it is not the primary responsibility of the supervisor to evaluate the contractor's performance, they may play a significant role in facilitating this process. This is achieved by cooperating with inspections and performance evaluations, providing the COR and CO with efficiency and productivity data, preparing formal reports on observed deficiencies and shortfalls in the contractor's performance, and keeping the COR closely involved in the day-to-day productive process.

Note

1. For a helpful discussion concerning the potential risks of personal-services violations inherent in performance-based service acquisitions, see Edward Allen Friar, *Performance-Based Service Acquisition* (PBSA, A-76) and "Personal Services, A Cautionary Note," *Defense Acquisition Review Journal*, December 2004.

5

Taking Charge of the Blended Workforce

Tips for Government Supervisors

___

Supervising the Government-Contractor Workplace

A PRINCIPLE CHALLENGE for many government supervisors leading blended workforces is adjusting to an entirely different set of rules, expectations, and obligations for dealing with contractor employees. Unlike a leader's normal obligations to a government team, supervisors have no direct responsibility for, authority over, or accountability to contractor employees. The government supervisor neither directs nor supervises the work of the contractor, nor should they become involved in the company's management of their employees. Government supervisors cannot request that contractor employees perform tasks or services that are not already explicitly enumerated in the agreement. Neither can government supervisors offer independent interpretations regarding the scope of work nor provide substantive modification to the tasks, outputs, or processes defined by the requirements statement. Additionally, government supervisors are not responsible for training and mentoring company employees, evaluating individual performance, or dealing with disciplinary matters, rewards, incentives, or other responsibilities typically under the purview of government managers. All of these issues are entirely the prerogative of the vendor's management team and designated site manager.

This restrictive mandate can be a difficult adjustment for leaders unfamiliar with the nature of the government-contractor relationship, but it is critically important that supervisors adhere to strict protocols for dealing with contractor employees. The paradox of supervising the blended workforce is that many of the practices and techniques essential to effective leadership of government teams are not appropriate when dealing with contractor employees. It is natural for government leaders to want to build their teams without drawing distinctions between employees, but this approach inevitably leads to conflicts of interest when applied to a blended government-contractor workforce. Treating contractor employees in the same manner as government employees violates the basic principles of the relationship and exposes supervisors to potential violations of acquisition regulation, prohibitions against personal services, and scope-of-work concerns. Maintaining a proper distinction between government and contractor employees is essential for preserving the integrity of the contract relationship.

A second challenge for government supervisors is adjusting to the cultural differences between the government and the commercial world. Supervisors must recognize that there are different values, objectives, imperatives, goals, priorities, languages, and expectations that distinguish the government from commercial workforces. By definition, commercial vendors do not share the same goals or objectives as the government supervisor beyond those specific tasks and requirements enumerated in the contract. It is important to remember that commercial vendors are providers of services and products to the government for the express purpose of earning profits to satisfy their shareholders. However well-meaning an individual contractor may be, supervisors should not conflate the vendor's efforts with serving the public interest. Contractors act on their own behalf for the purpose of private profit. This reality does not necessarily place contractors in conflict with the goals and interests of the government. Both sides provide essential services to the taxpayer. But the situation does necessitate a rules-based relationship to ensure efficiency and preserve the integrity of the cooperative partnership.

Taking Charge of the Blended Team: Basic Tips for Getting Started

This chapter discusses some basic considerations intended to help the government supervisor better manage the government-contractor partnership. As the supervisor prepares to take charge of a blended team, there are a few basic rules of thumb that should be considered early on in order to facilitate the initial transition and maximize the potential of the relationship.

1. Establish a good relationship with the contracting officer's representative (COR). Communicate often and effectively. Integrate the COR into daily operations of the workplace as much as possible.

2. Do not manage the contractor workforce. Let the vendor supervise their people.

3. Read the contract right away. Understand the statement of work. Know the conditions and standards of delivery established by the contract. Be aware of what the contractor is expected to do and what they cannot do.

4. Understand the authorities of the key players. Know the "lanes in the road" for everyone involved in the contracting process. Understand the duties and responsibilities of the COR, the contracting officer, the government supervisor, the vendor's site manager, and the contractor employees.

5. Set the conditions for the contractor's success. Create an operating environment and develop a workflow process providing the contractor workforce with maximum latitude to optimize their efforts and achieve the government's goals.

6. Minimize distractions to the contractor workforce. Create efficiency in the government's workflow process and tasking mechanisms so that the contractor can focus their effort on the requirements outlined in the statement of work.

7. Integrate the COR and contracting officer as much as possible into the daily operations of the workplace. Help them understand the technical aspects of the government's requirements and how the workflow process functions.

8. Work with the COR to refine requirements. Help the acquisition team establish clear, transparent, and quantifiable standards in order to measure the efficiency, productivity, and quality of contractor output.

9. Do not become involved in the contractor's employer-employee relationship. Let the site manager handle all decisions regarding direction, management, supervision, and personnel actions relating to their workforce.

10. Work with the COR to develop effective systems for tracking, measuring, and documenting contractor performance.

11. Ensure that all performance feedback is properly documented and reported to the acquisition team. Provide recommendations on observed deficiencies. Identify elements of the contract that require modification. Communicate these recommendations to the COR and contracting officer.

12. Refine and document changes to the government's requirements as processes evolve. Note the need for any new contractor skills or training.

13. Provide training to all employees on the government-contractor relationship to ensure ethical conduct in the blended workplace.
14. Take all necessary steps to secure sensitive government information, procurement-related material, and proprietary data.
15. When in doubt, always go to the COR.

Managing Relations with the Contracting Officer's Representative (COR)

The COR-supervisor relationship is perhaps the most important element for ensuring a successful outcome to the government-contractor partnership. The COR is the supervisor's primary resource for resolving questions, problems, or concerns regarding the operation and performance of the contractor workforce. Additionally, the COR will help the supervisor understand his or her role, authorities, and limitations with regard to management of the workforce and in resolving disputes relating to the contractor's work.

It is critically important that the supervisor establish good communication with the COR as soon as possible. Meeting with the COR should be the first priority for a new supervisor taking charge of a blended government-contractor workforce. Below is a list of key issues that should be on the agenda during the supervisor's first meeting with the COR.

1. Begin the process by jointly reviewing the contract and statement of work. The COR should be able to clearly explain all technical aspects of the contract, including the allowable scope of work and any limitations on the contractor's support of which the supervisor should be aware.
2. Have the COR explain the legal chain of authority, roles, and responsibilities of all players on the acquisition team.
3. During the discussion the supervisor should carefully describe their understanding of the organization's operations. This should include a description of the organizational structure, workflow-management systems, how requirements are relayed to the contractor workforce, and the nature of the goods or services delivered by the vendor. This conversation should ensure that both parties have a common understanding of the organization's operations and enable a substantive discussion of how the contractor will contribute to that process. Supervisors should not assume that the COR will have detailed knowledge about every aspect of the organization's product, processes, or structure. CORs are there to oversee administration of the contract but should not be expected to be technical experts in specific elements of the government's operation. The supervisor plays an important

role in educating the COR about these operations so that the COR can better communicate the government's requirements back to the contracting officer.

4. Once there is common understanding of the government's operation, the COR and supervisor should discuss how the contractor contributes to the process, what specific tasks they perform, and how they interface with their government counterparts. The COR should explain how the government-contractor relationship should function, including the mechanisms for tasking requirements to contractors and how the government will monitor and document feedback on their performance.

5. The COR should review any applicable limitations on the contractor's work. This may include such things as allowable man-hours, types of services, limitations of the contract, and legal, ethical, or security restrictions on functions that the contractor employees may perform or may include other restrictions that will impact how the supervisor manages the operations of the workforce.

6. The COR should describe the contract-surveillance plan and methodology for how oversight and performance monitoring will be conducted. The supervisor must ensure that he or she fully understands the details of the surveillance plan and how the COR intends to measure, assess, and document the contractor's performance. The COR should also discuss his or her expectations for how the supervisor will assist in this process. This may include such functions as providing informal performance feedback, workforce efficiency measures, output metrics, or facilitating routine inspections of the contractor's work.

7. The COR should identify all performance metrics and standards of delivery that will be used to evaluate the quality and efficiency of the contractor's process. If these measures are not clearly articulated, the supervisor should work with the COR and contracting officer to develop these standards.

8. The COR should discuss the methodology for documenting contractor performance. He or she should address how performance will be evaluated, the desired format and frequency of reports, and the terms of measure. The COR should identify what feedback, if any, is required from the government supervisor and what role the supervisor will play in monitoring and gathering performance data. In circumstances in which the COR is not physically located at the site of performance or for other reasons cannot be present to conduct continuous evaluation of the contractor's performance, the supervisor needs to know what aspects of the surveillance role will be delegated to COTRs or other oversight personnel.

9. Discuss with the COR what role the vendor will play in implementing internal quality control measures, periodic self-assessments, and monitoring of their employees. The supervisor should understand their role in this process as well as any requirement for conducting joint periodic performance reviews with the entire acquisition team, including the vendor's site manager.

10. Discuss the procedure for requesting modification to the workflow process or changes to the tasks assigned to the contractor. Discuss how changes to the contractor's assigned tasks may be requested and implemented, also when and how modifications to the contract language can be implemented if required.

11. Discuss the steps for remediation of deficiencies and shortfalls in contractor performance. The COR should explain the appropriate procedure for requesting changes in the contractor's performance and remediation steps to ensure that they happen.

12. Discuss with the COR the appropriate methods for government supervisors and employees to communicate instructions and specific tasking requirements to contractor employees. The COR should be able to clarify the appropriate limits and procedures for how work instructions will be relayed to the contractor. The COR should describe how minor corrections or clarifying input should be communicated to the contractor in order to facilitate the daily workflow process. The COR should also establish the threshold for when changes to requirements are significant enough that they must be brought to the attention of the COR or the contracting officer. It is important that the supervisor and COR develop a common understanding for how these inputs into the contractor's process will be addressed and handled.

13. In addition to meeting with the COR, it is also important for new supervisors to meet with the agency or departmental ethics and legal advisor to review organizational policies and rules concerning government-contractor relations. If possible, schedule a training session with the ethics advisor for all government employees in order to address potential questions and concerns that may arise in the workplace.

14. It is also helpful to meet with the contracting officer to discuss the overall contract-administration process. Although many contract-administration functions may be beyond the purview of the government supervisor, oftentimes the acquisition team will want to solicit their input. Supervisors have a great deal to offer the acquisition process due to their unique technical knowledge and firsthand experience with the government's requirements and processes. Other issues of interest that should be discussed with the CO include any new develop-

ments in the acquisition plan, proposed modifications to the contract language, upcoming rebids or contract-renewal options, and policy and budgetary changes that may effect the operation of the combined workforce. In some cases the acquisition team may be far removed from the actual site of contract performance and lack detailed technical knowledge of the process and day-to-day needs of the government. Close collaboration and feedback between the supervisor and the acquisition team is the best method for ensuring that the contract will be properly executed and that future contracts will be well-written and accurately reflect the government's changing requirements and needs.

Tips for Workforce Integration and Teambuilding

Experienced government managers are well aware of the importance of integrating new employees into cohesive teams. The first few days on the job create a lasting impression and set the tone for how new employees approach their work and interaction with the team. Government organizations go to great lengths to ensure that new employees are properly welcomed, trained on standards, and effectively integrated into operations. This process typically includes more than simply checking through the human resources department. A good manager will take the time to personally welcome all new employees, provide them an overview of operations, discuss standards of performance and expectations for behavior, and ensure that they receive all training, equipment, and instructions necessary to begin their work.

Generally speaking, service contracts will not stipulate detailed requirements for integrating new contractor employees. In most cases the vendor's site lead will bear responsibility for assisting his or her employees during their transition and integration into the government's operation. Nevertheless, supervisors should still consider developing a formal program for welcoming contractor employees onto the team. This effort will pay dividends in terms of fostering greater workforce cooperation, increasing efficiency, and maximizing productivity.

Once contractor employees are settled into the organization, it is then necessary to integrate them into cohesive and seamless teams. For supervisors of mixed government-contractor workforces the concept of teambuilding may be a somewhat misleading concept. In the current acquisition-community jargon it is common to hear people speak of *blended workforces*. While team integration and cooperation are appropriate goals, it is necessary to recognize the danger in taking such characterizations too far. The term *blended workforce* is one that can lead to erroneous presumptions about the government-contractor relationship, confusing the nature of the supervisor's role and authorities over contractor personnel.

In reality, the workforce is never truly blended, in the sense that supervisors must always maintain distinct lines of separation in their management of employees. It is essential that the distinctions between government and contractor personnel remain unambiguous and inviolable. Government and contractor workers exist in separate and distinct spheres with regard to pay, privileges, responsibilities, legal obligations, hiring and firing decisions, training opportunities, performance incentives, disciplinary procedures, and ethical standards. Therefore, when developing techniques for teambuilding it is imperative that supervisors devise strategies that respect and reinforce the integrity of the contractor-government relationship.

That being said, teambuilding within the blended workplace can and should occur within an appropriately defined sphere. These efforts will enhance the government-contractor partnership, resulting in improved efficiency and better performance of the workforce. The tips below offer some general ideas for facilitating integration of contractor employees into the government organizations and building productive government-contractor teams.

1. *Develop a checklist of contractor in-processing requirements.* Most organizations have extensive checklists of required events, briefings and training for new government employees. Although contractors will likely have very different requirements than new government hires, there should still be a similar list of items that each contractor should accomplish when they arrive at a new organization. At a minimum the list should include such things as procedures for obtaining badges and security credentials, computer-systems access, parking spots, workspace assignment, office supplies, et cetera. Site managers are responsible for ensuring that their employees accomplish these tasks, but it is up to the government supervisor to determine what requirements are necessary to properly integrate new contractors into the organization.

2. *Provide an organizational overview and mission briefing.* It is common for new government employees to receive an organizational welcome and overview briefing from a supervisor or senior executive. These meetings are helpful for setting the tone for leadership, communicating organizational values, defining the workplace identity and culture, and establishing expectations for performance and standards of behavior. These overview briefings also help new employees to understand how they fit into the mission and how their work contributes to the overall success of the larger organization. Although contractor employees are sometimes viewed as replaceable cogs in the machine, there is great ben-

efit in conveying a sense of how their work contributes to the big picture. This holistic knowledge is not only likely to help them understand the significance of their contributions to the government's operation but also creates opportunities for collaboration and synergy of effort on government-contractor teams. Supervisors should not overlook the potential value of contractor knowledge and experience, particularly as they are able to bring best practices from the private sector and other organizations into the government workplace. By providing contractor employees with a solid understanding of the organization's mission and process they will be better able to offer meaningful contributions to the government's efforts.

3. *Explain workflow procedures and standards of performance.* Just as it is important to provide new contractor employees with a macro-level overview of the organization's mission and functions, it is equally important to provide them with an understanding of the government team's workflow-management systems, production process, and quality control standards.

4. *Provide administrative guides, formats, and references.* Supervisors should carefully consider what guides, resources, and formatting examples a new contractor employee requires in order to begin functioning as part of the government team. The site manager should be provided with all relevant documents, formats, and references and should be tasked with training all new contractor employees in the required standards.

5. *Describe workplace rules and expectations.* Although not all government regulations apply to the contractor workforce, it is important that those common standards and expectations be clearly communicated to new contractor employees. This should be considered a preemptive effort to avoid uncomfortable confrontations later on by ensuring that contractor employees are aware of expected standards of behavior in the workplace. Examples of issues include such things as sexual-harassment policies, standards of workplace dress, appropriate use of titles for addressing senior executives and coworkers, policies on personal items in the office space, or even rules about keeping food items in the refrigerator. Although some of these issues seem rather banal, they are fertile seedbeds for distracting workplace drama. It is important for supervisors to communicate early to the contractor workforce that they are expected to abide by the same standards of behavior as their government counterparts. It is best not to leave contractors guessing which policies and expectations apply to them and which apply only to government employees.

6. *Detail security policies and procedures.* Contractor employees should not necessarily be expected to be familiar with government policies and

procedures for security, classification rules, and procedures for safe-guarding sensitive information. If a contractor's work involves classified material or sensitive information, government supervisors and site leaders must ensure that employees receive proper training on appropriate policies and procedures. Such issues may include facility-security requirements; use of government classification markings; information-systems security; classified material–handling procedures; courier operations; policies on the use of external-memory devices, cell phones, cameras, and recordable media in the workplace; and the use of government e-mail for personal business and correspondence. In some circumstances contractors will also require training on specialized equipment such as secure telephones, faxes, sensitive-material destruction procedures, or operation of classified computer networks. If contractors work on sensitive classified programs it may also be necessary for them to receive training on counterintelligence threats and policies relating to the protection of classified government information.

7. *Determine initial training requirements and continuing-education needs.* In most circumstances, the vendor bears responsibility for all training requirements for their employees. Well-written contracts should explicitly state the skills and prerequisites required for contractor employees. It should not fall to the government to provide additional training when a contractor employee fails to satisfy the minimum standards of performance. Nevertheless, there are situations in which contractor attendance at government-sponsored training events may positively benefit the government, aid in achievement of organizational goals, and bring greater efficiency to the workforce. If contractor participation in such training will clearly enhance the government's operation, a supervisor should discuss contractor-training options with the COR. In some cases the government may provide training to contractor employees if the government supervisor and vendor agree that training is appropriate and does not create a conflict of interest. Continuing education and training of the combined government-contractor workforce may also be required in instances where an organization institutes changes in policies and procedures or upgrades technology or other operating systems. Many government-sponsored schools and courses will permit contractor-employee attendance, particularly in cases where the vendor agrees to pay for the costs of training their employees. Such opportunities can provide value for both the company and the government when all members of the team share in the benefit of collective training.

8. *Provide combined training on government-contractor relations.* Just as government employees must be educated on ethical, legal, and conflict-

of-interest issues concerning government-contractor relations, contractor employees should also be aware of these issues as they pertain to their conduct in the government workplace. Supervisors should consider including contractors in their organization's annual ethics and legal training. A combined training program will foster a sense of collective obligation for maintaining a positive ethical and legal climate in the blended workplace.

9. *Foster collaboration and input from the contractor workforce.* Too often government organizations treat contractor service as piecework labor or assembly-line production. This is due partly to the fact that contractors are usually hired for a narrowly defined range of tasks. Supervisors are rightfully wary of asking them to do anything beyond the strict letter of the contract. Nevertheless, exposing contractor support to various elements of the organizational process can offer benefits and create flexibility within the workforce. Supervisors should consider working with the vendor to permit their employees to work on different projects or processes, provided that these tasks fall within the allowable scope of work. Many statements of work for general operational-support functions will permit some degree of latitude for rotating contractors to various functions within a government organization and permit work on different projects. Cross-training on different tasks and requirements is just as important for contractors as for government employees. This broadening of experience will infuse an organization with greater potential for innovation and add the flexibility to adjust operations as new employees are integrated into the team or when production requirements change. The ability to create diverse project teams including both government and contractor support will often enhance collaboration and bring new ideas to the government's process. It is important to remember that any such effort must be done in consultation with the COR and vendor's site manager so as not to violate the scope of work and terms of the contract.

10. *Provide feedback to the contractor workforce.* Regularly scheduled performance-review meetings with the COR and vendor site leader provide opportunities to review the progress and performance of the contractor workforce. There is a tendency to wait until problems arise before sitting down to discuss contractor performance, but supervisors should make feedback to the COR and vendor a regular part of their operational rhythm. The team will benefit from habitual opportunities to review overall progress and performance levels. During these scheduled meetings, the supervisor and COR can recommend

adjustments to the workflow process and operations to improve quality and efficiency. Scheduled reviews also provide the opportunity to discuss administrative matters, personnel turnover, or training issues that may impact the organization's operation.

11. *Request contractor self-assessments.* Performance assessment of the contractor workforce should not be a one-way street. The natural inclination for government supervisors is to identify problems and present solutions, but it is equally important to solicit advice and recommendations from the contractor workforce. This seems like a self-evident recommendation, but it is one that is frequently forgotten. Government supervisors tend to take ownership for the processes they manage and are often too quick to devise solutions without consulting the contractor for advice or recommendation. One way to ensure that this occurs is to request that the contractor perform periodic self-assessments, including feedback on how their operations are integrated into the larger government process. This process will serve as a forcing mechanism to ensure that the contractor becomes an active participant and partner in identifying process deficiencies and proposing solutions to improve their support to the government operation.

12. *Work to minimize personnel turnover.* Government supervisors sometimes tend to view contractor personnel as generic cogs in their productive process. In some respects this is a healthy outlook, in that government organizations should never become so dependent on an individual contractor that their operations are significantly jeopardized by turnover. But there is also a problem in presuming that contractor personnel are easily replaceable without adverse impact on government operations. Frequent personnel turnover, government or contractor, puts enormous strain on an organization, eroding the human-capital base and disrupting efficiency of the workflow process. Government supervisors should communicate frequently with the vendor's program managers on key personnel changes. Although the government supervisor should not become involved in the vendor's personnel-management decisions, they must still be aware of personnel movements and how these changes impact the organization. Government supervisors should work with the vendor to minimize unprogrammed contractor personnel changeover. Frequent transitions, and subsequent requirements for retraining new personnel, place enormous strain on the government's operation, leading to inefficiency, problems with workforce integration, and poor performance of the team.

13. *Help the site manager reward and recognize their people.* It is important to remember that under no circumstances should a gov-

ernment supervisor become involved in advocating or directing performance-related awards to contractor employees. Ultimately it is the responsibility of the vendor to create performance incentives for their employees and reward good work. Nevertheless, if an individual contractor or government-contractor team delivers exceptional performance, it is important that the supervisor communicate this feedback to the COR and vendor through the formal feedback process. It is important to recognize, document, and report good contractor performance as well as deficiencies. This effort by the supervisor will help the contractor improve and refine their operations and in the end return benefit to the government, as the contractor is able to provide improved support.

Reading the Contract: What the Supervisor Needs to Know

One of the primary objectives of the supervisor's first meeting with the COR should be review and discussion of the contract. This will provide the supervisor with the opportunity to clarify any questions or concerns regarding the contract and ensure mutual understanding of the government's objectives and the vendor's obligations. It is a disturbing reality that many government supervisors with contractors operating in their workplace do not actually take the time to read the contract governing the activities of these employees. There is absolutely no substitute for a supervisor reading the contract and having familiarity with the terms of the agreement.

The contract provides the supervisor with critical knowledge about the terms of the statement of work, standards of delivery, metrics to quantify success, contract-administration procedures, and the government's surveillance plan. It is not necessary that the supervisor become an expert in contracting or mastering every last detail of the acquisition process, but it is important to read and understand the terms of the agreement to ensure a productive partnership. This knowledge will help avoid problems and disputes before they happen and reduce the potential for misunderstandings and violations of the agreement.

Understanding the Statement of Work

If the supervisor focuses on one thing, it should be the contract's statement of work (SOW). From the supervisor's perspective, this is the critical element of the agreement. The statement of work defines the government's requirement and establishes the contractor's obligation. It explains precisely what work the contractor must accomplish and the standards for delivery and performance. Essentially, it explains everything that the contractor is expected to do in the workplace.

The SOW should be the supervisor's primary reference document for understanding how the contractor contributes to the government's operation. It is the basis for resolving any disputes between the government and vendor. A good understanding of the SOW will enable the supervisor to better communicate with the COR and the vendor's management team in order to maximize efficiency and performance. For these reasons it is important that the supervisor possess a basic understanding of the key elements of a well-written statement of work.

The Purpose of the Statement of Work

The statement of work sets the basic terms for a successful contract agreement. The SOW provides important information for both the contractor and the government. It should reflect the government's understanding of the contract's objectives and standards for performance. From the start of the acquisition process the SOW establishes parameters for conducting market search, managing the solicitation, and conducting the source-selection process. The team will evaluate vendor proposals against the requirements expressed in the SOW and select the best alternative based on these criteria.

A well-written SOW should be clear, direct, and easily interpreted by any reader. If the language is confusing or standards unclear it will inevitably create confusion and disputes between the government and the contractor. It should have sufficient detail to enable a vendor to develop accurate proposals, cost estimates, work plans, and personnel selection.

Once the contract is awarded and work begins, the SOW becomes the basis for establishing the contractor's performance requirements and expectations. The SOW establishes terms of reference for effective contract administration, oversight, and contract surveillance. The SOW also contains other information relevant to the execution of the contract, including matters relating to work conditions, employee qualifications, training requirements, performance standards, evaluation criteria, inspection schedules, work hours, specified and implied tasks, legal restrictions, clearance requirements, provisions for use of government property and equipment, and other special requirements and instructions.

There is no set formula for development of a statement of work, but there are some basic elements common in most contracts. At a minimum, the SOW should address the following items relating to the contractor's work.

- *Scope of work.* Describes the nature of the work to be performed, including work plan, required deliverables, and performance standards.
- *Period of performance.* Provides a start and end date for the project and any other items relating to scheduling, milestones, and delivery timelines.
- *Location of performance.* Describes the place where the work will be performed. This may also include any relevant information on the environmental conditions of performance. This is particularly important for contingency contracting or contractor work occurring in deployed locations.
- *Supplies, material, and equipment.* Lists all supplies and equipment that will be used in execution of the contract. It is important to distinguish government-furnished equipment versus materials that must be provided by the contractor.
- *Payment rate.* Describes cost estimates and the dollar amount for all goods and services. May also include the total dollar amount of the award and explanation of the payment schedule, incentive structure, or other matters relating to cost reimbursement.
- *Delivery standards.* Describes the expected quality level and standards of delivery that will determine if a product or service is acceptable to the government.
- *Other special requirements.* Addresses any special aspects of the requirement, including hardware or software requirements, specialized workforce skills, mandatory training or certifications for contractor personnel, travel requirements, safety and/or security requirements, and anything else not covered in the contract.

Other Things to Look for in the Contract

When a new supervisor first takes charge of the blended workforce they should start by reviewing all terms of the contract. Below are some more specific issues that the government supervisor should be aware of when reviewing the statement of work and contract language.

- *General contract scope and overall objective.* Supervisors must be aware of the overall objective of the contract. They should have a clear understanding of the goods or services that the vendor is tasked to provide.
- *Position descriptions, scope of duties, and specific work requirements.* The contract should provide a description of the general scope of duties to be performed by the contractor employees. This section should enumerate specific tasks and functions that contractors will perform as well as any

constraints or limitations on the scope of their activities. It is important for supervisors to be familiar with the position descriptions and task requirements to ensure that contractors employed in their workplace are not asked to do any duties or tasks outside the scope of the requirement. Scope-of-work violations are one of the more common problems in the hybrid workplace, particularly with government employees or supervisors unfamiliar with the requirements language and terms of the contract. Generally speaking, inadvertent or minor violations of scope of work can be easily resolved between the supervisor, the COR, and the vendor's site manager, but habitual tasking of contractors for performance of work outside the contract requirements could constitute an unauthorized obligation and possibly expose the government to a legal claim by the vendor. A knowledgeable supervisor, familiar with the contract language, is the most effective protection against these possible violations.

- *Referenced regulations, forms, technical manuals, and policy letters.* Be aware of specific government directives, guidelines, regulations, or manuals that are referenced in the contract language. These may describe the nature of the services or goods provided, give references for standards of delivery or performance, or provide legal limitations and guidelines on the nature of work provided by the contractor. Supervisors should always maintain a copy on hand of any document, manual, or regulation referenced in the contract. These reference documents may be critical to understanding any implied standards of performance or stipulations applying to the contractor's work.
- *Contractor skills and prerequisites.* If a contract provides primarily services, note any references to special skill sets, security-clearance requirements, or prerequisite training required of the contractor workforce. This knowledge is important for several reasons: First, it is a safeguard for the government if the vendor assigns an employee to a task for which they do not possess the prerequisites or training. Second, it is the government supervisor's responsibility to optimize the workflow process and make determinations about allocation of resources. This includes leveraging unique contractor skills, experience, and training. While the government supervisor should not direct the assignment of individual contractors, he or she should be aware of the general qualifications of the contractor workforce so as to be able to make an appropriate determination about overall operations. The supervisor can then work in cooperation with the vendor's management team to ensure the optimal allocation and assignment of contractor personnel.
- *Hours of operation, leave, holiday, and sick day policy.* Although these issues are managed directly by the vendor's site manager, it is important

for the supervisor to understand the general terms of work in order to make informed resource decisions regarding allocations of the contractor's labor. Supervisors must build their own process requirements and delivery schedules based on accurate assumptions of actual available man-hours that the contractor will provide. The supervisor should be aware of factors such as contractor vacation, holiday periods, and sick leaves that may impact government planning, resourcing, and allocation of labor for the completion of projects.

- *Work conditions and special requirements.* Supervisors should take note of any special requirements that may impact the employment of assigned-contractor support. This may include special conditions of the work environment, mandated training requirements, tools or equipment provided to the contractor, and stipulations on issues such as overtime requests or procedures for requesting additional contractor support. These issues are particularly important if the contract stipulates special terms for work performed in deployed locations or contingency environments. Government supervisors must be particularly aware of any potential conditions that place limitations on the contractor's performance of their assigned duties. These may be related to security, safety, environmental conditions, work-hour limitations, or other factors limiting the utilization of contractor support.

- *Period of performance.* This issue is particularly important if the contract is coming up for renewal, extension, or rebid. These events are natural junctures in the acquisition process where the supervisor can provide important feedback to the COR and the contracting officer concerning contractor performance or suggested modifications to the contract language. A contract renewal or rebid process offers the government an opportunity to negotiate modifications in the scope of work to reflect changes in the government's requirements or the inclusion of additional provisions to the original contract. These transitions should be used as an opportunity to review or revise the requirements analysis and determine if the current contract language still reflects the actual nature of the government's needs. Additionally, the supervisor can determine if the skills and training of the contractor workforce is adequate to the demands of the operation. The period of performance also comes into play if there is uncertainty about the prospect of contract renewal. The supervisor should be cautious about making planning assumptions for major projects or operations if the plan depends on specific contributions of the contractor workforce. A contract nonrenewal or an award to a new vendor will have significant impact on the efficiency and quality of the government's operation during the transition period. Supervisors must take these variables into account as they conduct strategic planning for their organizations.

- *Security concerns.* Security issues may be particularly important if contractors are involved in work on classified programs or sensitive material. Supervisors must be aware of any explicit restrictions on contractor access to certain information in their workplace, as well as the security-clearance levels of the entire contract workforce. Contractor employees should not be assigned to a restricted or classified work environment without appropriate clearances, but it is still the supervisor's responsibility to manage workplace access so that the contractor workforce only has access to government information that is relevant to the performance of their contractual duties. Supervisors must be aware of what the contractors need to know and what information is beyond the scope of their duties and plan accordingly.
- *Special legal requirements.* Supervisors should review the contract for any special legal concerns or stipulations that may affect the function of the contractor workforce. Some contracts for services in deployed locations or in support of contingency operations outside the United States may have unique stipulations concerning contractor legal rights in the host country or liabilities under the Uniform Code of Military Justice (UCMJ) or Military Extraterritorial Jurisdiction Act (MEJA). Supervisors should be generally familiar with special legal considerations that may impact the operation of their workforce, particularly if performing certain functions may place the contract workforce or government at increased legal risk.
- *Standards of conduct.* Supervisors should review the contract language for any stipulations on contractor conduct in the workplace. Beyond what is written in the contract, supervisors do have some latitude-setting workplace standards of behavior and conduct but should check with the COR or legal advisor to determine the exact applicability to the contractor workforce. For contractors working in forward locations supporting contingency operations, contracts may contain special guidance on such concerns as use of weapons, alcohol consumption, or social relations with local nationals and government employees. The vendor's site leader is primarily responsible for enforcing the lawful and proper conduct of their employees. They will also handle minor disciplinary matters as they arise, but supervisors should still be aware of what restrictions are outlined in the contract and how these stipulations may affect workplace operations.
- *Policy for replacement of personnel.* Be aware of the policy or procedures for the removal or replacement of contractor personnel. Although the

COR and site leader will directly handle these issues, the government supervisor should be aware of the contractual requirements and estimated timeline for personnel replacement. These actions could potentially affect resource-allocation decisions in the event that a contractor is removed from the site of performance. Supervisors must take these considerations into account when developing their management assumptions.

- *Special security requirements and nondisclosure agreements.* These issues are particularly important if contractors are working with classified programs, sensitive data, proprietary information, or in support of intelligence or law-enforcement activities. Supervisors must ensure that their organization's process takes into account the impact of implementing special security requirements and safeguarding government information.

- *Medical support, life support, housing, food, and transportation.* These issues primarily concern contractor work in remote locations or contingency environments. Although government supervisors will most likely not be responsible for coordinating these issues, their implementation does have an impact on the availability and scheduling of the contractor's work. For this reason, supervisors must understand how these terms of the contract will affect planning, resource allocation, and the availability of the contractor's labor. Operational plans must take into account any unique stipulations for sustainment and life-support needs of the workforce that will affect the government's workflow process and impact contractor performance.

- *Quality control plan.* When reviewing the contract, the supervisor should pay close attention to any requirements relating to the vendor's internal quality control plan. Particular attention should be directed to the methodology and standards that the vendor will apply to the oversight and quality control of their employees' work. It is important that these standards and expectations conform to the government's requirements and the supervisor's expectations. It should be immediately apparent to the supervisor if the contractor delivers goods or services that do not satisfy the standards outlined in the quality control plan. Supervisors must remember that it is the job of the vendor's management team to ensure that their employees deliver work to the government on time and to standard. The purpose of the quality control plan is to ensure that this happens with minimal government oversight and intervention.

- *Inspection schedules, methodologies, and reporting requirements.* Supervisors should review the contract to ensure that they have a firm understanding of the requirements for monitoring work, conducting inspections, and documenting and reporting contractor performance. Supervisors should review the plan with the COR and discuss surveillance methodology and

how the procedures will be conducted. Ideally, the COR will be sufficiently integrated into the daily operations so that he or she is able to conduct a significant degree of the surveillance in person. It is important that
supervisors assist in this effort, particularly in situations when the COR is
not physically present at the site of performance. In such circumstances
a COTR or designated representative becomes the COR's eyes and ears,
playing a cooperative role to ensure that performance inspections, surveillance, and periodic assessments are completed and documented.

- *Government-furnished property, services, equipment, or training.* Some
  contracts will stipulate specific requirements for equipment or property
  that must be supplied to the contractor workforce by the government.
  Supervisors must be aware of these requirements so as to ensure that the
  workforce is supplied with all materials necessary to complete their tasks.
  This may include such items as computers, office space, office supplies,
  systems training, reference materials, network access, and other tools
  necessary for the contractor to complete all required tasks. The COR
  should take the active lead in overseeing this, but the supervisor needs to
  be aware of the requirements for their team so that they can identify any
  deficiencies or shortfalls.
- *Vendor-furnished property, services, and equipment.* Just as the supervisor should be aware of what materials the government must provide to
  the contractor, they should also be aware of contract clauses relating to
  vendor-supplied property, equipment, or training. This is particularly
  true if delivery of goods or services depends on the vendor's supply
  of these materials. Failure of the vendor to complete work due shortfalls
  in these areas would reflect in an unexcused delay on the part of the contractor, which should be reflected in the performance evaluation.
- *Administration and record-keeping.* Supervisors should be aware of any
  special administrative requirements. Generally speaking, the vendor
  assumes responsibility for all record-keeping functions relating to
  their employees, such as time cards, medical records, credentialing,
  performance records, and security-clearance files. Vendors should also
  maintain purchase records for items not provided by the government
  but required for performance of their duties. Many contracts will also
  stipulate requirements for contractors to maintain records of quality-
  control inspections. It is the responsibility of the COR to ensure that
  these activities are occurring, but supervisors should be aware of the
  requirements and the process.
- *Contractor-training requirements.* It is important that the supervisor read
  the contract for stipulations concerning contractor training. In some
  cases, contractor employees may not have received all of the required

training before beginning a job or may not be immediately prepared to perform their tasks according to the government's standard. This is particularly the case if the government's production requirements do not conform to an equivalent commercial standard or if the production requirements involve use of unfamiliar technology, networks, automations tools, regulatory guidance, or policy rules that must be learned on the job. In such cases, it is important for supervisors to understand which party bears responsibility for providing the remedial training to transition the contractor into the government's operations. In most cases, the requirement for providing additional training will fall to the vendor, but the contract may stipulate options for certain government-provided courses, continuing education, or refresher training that can be made available to contractor employees to assist them in performance of their duties. The supervisor should be aware of what is and what is not provided for in the contract.

- *Policy for corrective actions and resolution of disputes.* The COR should always be the supervisor's primary resource for resolving any disputes with the vendor concerning interpretation of the contract or issues with standards of delivery. Nevertheless, the supervisor should review the contract for any language concerning how disputes will be handled. It is also important to review clauses relating to the removal of a contractor for cause. While the supervisor is not authorized to independently make these determinations, they should be aware of how removal or replacement of a contractor is handled and how it effects their operations and productivity.

- *Contractor qualifications.* It is important that supervisors understand the resources and inputs to their process. In the case of service-based contracts, the inputs are the skill, experience, and qualifications of the vendor's employees. Therefore, it is important for the supervisor to pay particular attention to how the contract describes the qualifications required of the contractor workforce. This knowledge is critically important in developing a plan for integrating contractor personnel and applying their skills to appropriate tasks in the government's process. To optimize the efficiency of a process the government supervisor must be able to accurately assess the capabilities, strengths, and weaknesses of the contractor workforce. The contract should provide some information on basic job prerequisites that will provide the supervisor some idea about the expected qualifications, skills, and experience of the workforce. Unfortunately, there will also be times when a vendor provides employees who do not fully meet the needs of the government or terms of the agreement. The supervisor must be aware of all mandatory prerequisites in order to identify to the COR any individuals whose performance, skills, or training do not satisfy the requirements established by the contract. Some contracts will stipulate that employee résumés be supplied in advance to the contracting officer for review, but this is not always the case. It is also important to remember that for contracts supporting contingency operations or in forward-deployed locations there will frequently be additional medical requirements for contractor employees, such as health screenings and immunizations. It is the responsibility of the COR and the vendor to ensure that all contractor employees arriving on the job site are fully qualified according to the terms and conditions of the contract.

- *Vendor responsibilities.* Many contracts will outline specific duties to be performed by the vendor's site manager. These may include the development and implementation of a quality control plan (QCP) and an inspection schedule. There may also be some provisions concerning how the site manager will resolve disputes over work performance, disciplinary actions, ethical violations, or other matters relating to their employees. While it is not the responsibility of the government supervisor to oversee any of these functions, it is still helpful to be aware of the expectations and requirements for the vendor's management team.

6

Managing the Blended Workforce

Ethical, Legal, and Security Concerns

Managing the Government-Contractor Workforce:
Ethical and Legal Concerns

THERE WILL BE INSTANCES in which ethical and legal concerns arise in the supervisor's dealings with the contractor workforce. For this reason it is critical that the supervisor possess a solid understanding of the rules governing contractors in the workplace. It is the supervisor's responsibility to establish the ethical climate for the workforce. This requires that all employees, government and contractor alike, understand and respect the standards for ethical conduct in the workplace. This will help ensure that employees do not inadvertently engage in behavior that compromises the integrity of the government-contractor relationship.

This task can be more complicated than it seems. While government employees are subject to the rules of their agency, it is important to remember that contractor employees are not bound precisely by the same set of guidelines. Contractors are expected to abide by federal laws generally applicable to any citizen, as well as rules specific to the workplace where their tasks are performed if in a government facility. Beyond this, the behavior of contractor employees is defined primarily by the terms of the contract and internal policies of their company. In effect, this creates two operative standards for the single blended workforce. It is the supervisor's challenge to educate the workforce on these distinctions and implement a functional ethical climate that applies to all employees.

The tips below cover some particular areas of concern with regard to ethical and legal issues likely to arise in the blended workplace. They do not cover every potential situation and supervisors should be aware that these are general guidelines only. Specific questions regarding application of legal standards for each workplace should always be discussed with the COR and organizational legal advisor.

Establishing an Ethical Climate in the Government-Contractor Workplace

1. The most important rule of thumb for the supervisor is immediate reporting of incidents or suspicious activities in the workplace. Raise suspected violations of ethical or legal standards to the COR, contracting officer, organizational ethics counselor, or legal advisor as soon as possible.
2. Ensure that all government employees receive annual ethics training, including instruction on procurement integrity and rules for dealing with contractors in the workplace. A positive ethical and legal climate cannot be accomplished without an education and training program establishing the expectations that apply to the workforce.
3. Certain restrictions limiting political activities in the government workplace under the Hatch Act do not specifically apply to contractor employees. The Hatch Act and accompanying DOD regulations prohibit government personnel from conducting political activities in the workplace but are not uniformly applicable to nongovernment personnel. Agencies or organizations must establish separate workplace policies for contractors or, if necessary, include appropriate clauses in contract language to ensure that there is no confusion regarding political solicitation, fundraising, or other activities performed by contractors in the workplace.
4. Contractor employees may or may not be subject to similar restrictions and disciplinary measures relating to equal opportunity, sexual harassment, or drug or alcohol abuse. If the contract does not offer language regarding these issues, be sure to consult the organizational legal advisor for specific policy and guidelines as to the applicability of such rules to the contractor workforce.
5. Contractor employees may be afforded certain whistleblower protections for reporting ethical, regulatory, or security violations observed in the government workplace. Supervisors and the vendor's site manager should consult the organizational legal advisor to understand how these protections are afforded to contractor workforce under agency policy.

6. Supervisors should be aware of potential intellectual-property-rights concerns resulting from the collaborative efforts of government-contractor teams. As a general rule, the vendor retains certain commercial rights to intellectual designs, conceptual processes, software, or inventions created in collaboration with government personnel. Consult a legal advisor for specific questions concerning proprietary ownership of projects, designs, concepts, or data generated as a result of collaborative work.

7. Supervisors and government employees should not engage in discussions with contractors or vendor representatives concerning potential employment opportunities. This is a particular area of concern due to the significant numbers of government personnel departing jobs for the private sector, often returning as contractors to work in the same government offices and on similar projects as during the period of their federal service. Supervisors must educate their workforce on conflict-of-interest concerns and the appropriate rules for post-government employment with contractors working on projects within their agency or organization.

8. Contractors should not use the organization's name or symbol in connection with any services or goods provided by the company in such a manner that implies an authorized government endorsement.

9. Supervisors must be cognizant of using their position to influence a contractor or vendor for personal benefit or financial gain. Do not solicit or accept favors, gratuities, or other special benefits for yourself or family members from a contractor or vendor representative.

10. Government personnel are generally restricted from accepting gift items or compensation from what are considered *prohibited sources.* In simple terms, a prohibited source is any individual or organization potentially seeking official action on the part of a government official or agency, such as a contractor doing business with the organization. Supervisors should be aware that there are numerous exceptions to the general guideline regarding minor gifts or participation in contractor-sponsored events (see next tip). In all cases, it is best to consult the organizational ethics advisor for specific details and questions.

11. As a general rule supervisors should not accept gifts from vendors and contractor employees, but certain exceptions do apply based on factors such as total cash value (generally nothing more than $20), the existence of a personal relationship with the contractor, or minor gifts and refreshments served as part of a widely attended gathering or event open to the public. Transportation, food, and beverages

provided by vendors are also considered gifts under government ethics rules. Be aware that many vendor companies also have ethics codes that restrict their provision of gifts or services to government employees. Whenever in doubt with regard to the appropriateness of a specific gift or service, be sure to consult the organizational ethics or legal advisor for a definitive answer.

12. If a government supervisor accepts goods or services provided by the contractor for use, a receipt should be made reflecting the full market value. This transaction should be reported to the agency ethics advisor to ensure that it does not violate organizational guidelines.

13. Government supervisors should not mandate that contractor employees attend functions or parties that interfere with their assigned duties unless authorized by the vendor's management team. For government-sponsored office parties, contractors cannot use contract hours to attend these functions. Contractor use of billable work hours to attend government social functions is generally unauthorized, even if the function is an approved place of duty for government employees. Contractor attendance at such functions must be coordinated in advance with the supervisor, site manager, and COR. Arrangements must be made to account for nonworked hours in accordance with company policy.

14. Contractors should never be requested to sponsor, organize, or set up an official or nonofficial government function unless the contract language specifically authorizes their performance of these tasks. Contractors must not be compelled to provide funds or other forms of material support to these functions but may do so on a voluntary basis.

15. Government supervisors may attend contractor-sponsored social events, but certain restrictions apply. Supervisors may accept invitations, based on a bona fide personal relationship with a contractor employee, to events that are open to the public or widely attended by a specified category of government employee (i.e., an event open to all military personnel) or as a result of an invitation based on associations unrelated to a supervisor's status as a government employee. As with gifts, when in doubt it is best to consult the organizational ethics advisor for specific guidelines and limitations.

16. There are allowances for attendance of both government and contractor personnel at private and public parties, but supervisors should be aware of specific limitations and restrictions on the costs of meals, beverages, and entertainment. Additionally, any government funds allocated specifically for morale or welfare functions may not be used to support contractor attendance. This includes contractor use of government-funded tickets, subsidized meals, drinks, or entertain-

ment. For such events the vendor or employee is responsible for paying their own expenses.

17. Employees should be aware of prohibitions against soliciting contractor contributions for organizational parties and events. This applies to contractor or vendor contributions to such things as door prizes, gift certificates, or any other donated item. In circumstances such as an office potluck or holiday party, individual contractors may make contributions, but they must be entirely voluntary and solicited without pressure from the government supervisor.

18. Each organization should have established policies and restrictions on contractor use of government-owned vehicles and transportation benefits. In general, unless specifically authorized in the contract, a vendor's employees are typically not permitted to use government vehicles.

19. Certain restrictions may apply to informal office collections or solicitations for going-away gifts, baby showers, condolence flowers, or other group gifts for government or contractor personnel. Government supervisors cannot request contributions from contractor employees, since this is considered a solicitation from a prohibited source. This restriction even includes requesting contractor support for government-sponsored voluntary contributions, such as the Combined Federal Campaign. Contractors are free to make voluntary contributions, although some restrictions apply regarding the amount that they may contribute. Similar rules apply with regard to requesting funds for holiday gift parties, "secret Santa" exchanges, or other organized exchange of gifts, services, or money. Be sure to consult your ethics advisor for specific details on office gift giving in a blended workforce.

20. Supervisors and vendor site mangers should be aware of policies on the appropriate use of government-provided property. This includes such things as office space, telephones, computers, e-mail, transportation, morale or welfare services, and other forms of government-employee compensation and benefits. The contracting officer bears responsibility for determining the proper use of all government property by contractor personnel, but the COR should be able to offer necessary clarification as to contractor use of government-supplied equipment. Supervisors should also be aware of potential issues regarding contractor use of licensed software or applications purchased by the government for limited use on registered systems.

21. Generally speaking, a government supervisor should not work on a project with contractor partners if he or she has personal interests with the vendor, such as a spouse seeking employment with the contractor or significant financial involvement with the firm.

22. Ethics regulations prohibit government supervisors from participating in outside employment with a contractor with which they have official duties and interactions. This general rule also applies to other activities that may give the appearance of a government supervisor using association with the contractor for personal gain.

23. Government supervisors cannot represent or negotiate on behalf of a contractor who is providing support to their organization, even on issues unrelated to the particular tasks under their purview.

24. Ethics rules do not strictly prohibit dating or close personal relationships between government and contractor employees, but extreme caution should be used in any situation in which relations may give the appearance of favoritism or may compromise the impartiality of a government supervisor toward the performance of the contractor.

25. Government supervisors are generally prohibited from endorsing any product or service provided by a vendor. This restriction extends to any public statement or evaluation relating to the quality of a contractor's performance. There may be circumstances in which a contractor requests a letter of recommendation or job reference based on individual performance during their work on a particular government contract. These situations should be handled on a case-by-case situation, and supervisors should consult the organizational legal advisor for an appropriate determination.

26. Certain legal and ethical restrictions apply to postgovernment employment with contractors. Government supervisors should immediately consult the organizational legal advisor if they chose to quit government service and seek employment with a contractor working on projects directly related to the government supervisor's official duties. As a general rule of thumb, government supervisors should never work on government matters involving contractors with whom they are seeking employment.

27. Certain conflict-of-interest rules apply to newly hired government employees limiting their association with contracts and the work of their former employer. This is particularly true in cases where a government supervisor may have significant continuing financial interests in a company, such as stock options or pension plans.

Security Best Practices for the Government-Contractor Workplace

It has become relatively common in recent years to see contractor employees working in environments where classified material or sensitive programs are handled. Significant numbers of contractors are employed in support of intelligence community programs, military operations, and other venues where they are exposed to materials and information with clearance requirements and access restrictions. Although all contractors should have appropriate security credentials prior to their assignment on classified government programs, it is still the responsibility of the supervisor to ensure that access to sensitive information and operations are appropriately controlled and monitored.

It is incumbent on the government supervisor to ensure that all processes and operating procedures in the government-contractor workplace adhere to appropriate security requirements and that contractors have access only to information required for the completion of their assigned tasks as described in the contract language. Simply because a contractor employee holds a particular security clearance does not justify their access to information unrelated to the scope of their proscribed duties under the contract. Access to information, programs, and systems should be specifically restricted to what is required for the performance of their tasks. It is incumbent on the government supervisor to establish office space layout and workforce procedures that facilitate appropriate security measures for contractors working in restricted-access or controlled facilities.

Supervisors must take into account a variety of security concerns, everything from proper badges and credentials to arranging for physical segregation of contractor employees when access to information must be limited. The tips below provide some issues of consideration for contractor employees working in environments where sensitive or classified information is handled and stored. These tips do not cover all situations and circumstances. It is important that the supervisor consult with the organizational security manager and the COR to develop internal policies and procedures for dealing with contractor employees working in classified government facilities.

1. Supervisors must ensure that contractors are properly cleared and credentialed and that their status as nongovernment employees is clearly identified at all times. There should never, under any circumstances, be confusion in a workplace as to who is a government employee and who is a contractor. Proper attention to badges, systems access, credentialing, and identification will ensure that appropriate lines of authority and security procedures are always maintained.
2. Exercise caution in any situation in which a contractor may have access to information relating to future contract bids, requests for proposal, new government requirements, acquisition budget projections, cost estimates, and contract performance evaluations or administrative documents relating to acquisition planning.

3. Consider the use of nondisclosure agreements in situations when contractors may have access to sensitive operational, intelligence, or proprietary information. At all times contractor access to such information must be weighed against a need-to-know standard. Government supervisors are obligated to establish policies and procedures to limit contractor access to information that is beyond the required scope of their duties.

4. Unless required by the nature of their assigned tasks, contractors should not have access to Privacy Act information or other sensitive nonpublic data that would ordinarily not be releasable under the Freedom of Information Act. Privacy information includes, but is not limited to, personal identifying information, social security numbers, payroll numbers, educational information, financial transactions, medical histories, results of drug testing, criminal records, and employment histories. The Privacy Act requires that this type of information be protected from unauthorized disclosure and establishes civil and criminal penalties for violations. Contractors may access Privacy Act information only when performing an authorized contract function requiring their access to this information. In such situations legal penalties for misuse or unauthorized disclosure of information applies to contractor personnel the same as it does for government employees. It is important to note that some privacy laws vary from state to state. Consult the organizational legal advisor on how these statutes may apply to each workplace and contract.

5. Make appropriate accommodations for physical security in the workplace. Supervisors must find an appropriate balance between fostering effective government-contractor collaboration and necessary measures to limit contractor access to information not required for their duties. In some cases security concerns may require spatial segregation of contractor and government workspaces.

6. Supervisors should consider employing security measures and controlled access to classified faxes and computer networks. This may include establishing network restrictions, access limitations, or file-sharing guards on government computer systems in order to limit contractor access to information unrelated to the performance of their duties.

7. Supervisors should establish appropriate need-to-know limitations on personnel attending meetings or briefings in which contractor attendance is required. Access should be determined by government program managers based on the required level of contractor participation.

8. Supervisors must ensure that contractors receive all necessary training on agency and organizational security policies. This may include such things as physical security practices, classification standards, security

markings, and procedures for transportation, storage, and safeguarding of sensitive information. Training should include instruction relating to security practices for telephone conversations, e-mail, Internet usage, and other forms of communication that could potentially compromise sensitive government information. Supervisors should never assume that the vendor company has provided training to their workforce on these issues. Contractor personnel must be trained to the same standards as their government counterparts on all security standards, practices, and procedures.

9. Supervisors should compartmentalize information as required. Consider disabling automation and network-systems externals to prevent unauthorized download of government information unless required by the contractor's assigned duties.

10. Limit access to organizational electronic share folders and digital communities of interest. Consider setting up separate data files on shared drives especially designated for contractor or company use. Network specialists can establish folders with access restrictions for government use only and others that are open-access for government-contractor collaborative projects.

11. Ensure that distribution chains for sensitive hardcopy and digital information are tightly controlled. Contractors should not be placed in situations where they have incidental access to such information.

12. Ensure that the organizational networks clearly distinguish between government and contractor employees. This should always include attaching distinctive e-mail address aliases to contractor employees. This will ensure that when government employees send group e-mails or reply to all of the addresses in an e-mail thread, they are clearly aware that contractor employees are listed on the receipt line.

13. When making determinations for contractor access to classified or sensitive information, supervisors should ask the following questions to ensure that the decision has been properly considered.

- Are there agency- or departmental-policy restrictions against this action? Have the appropriate policies and regulations been reviewed as part of the access determination?
- Does this action require outside legal or security review? Who is the final approval authority for access?
- Is the purpose for disclosing this information required within the scope of the duties enumerated in the contract?
- Does the contractor employee have a need to know?
- Does the contractor have appropriate security clearances to access the information?

- Are adequate safeguards in place to ensure that the contractor will not disclose or misuse the information?
- Has the contractor received all required training on use, handling, storage, and control of the information in question?
- Are necessary monitoring and safeguards established to assure appropriate use of the information?
- Is there a plan to terminate access when the contractor's use of the information is no longer required?

14. Supervisors must ensure that all government employees are aware of procedures for reporting suspected security violations relating to contractor employees. This implies that government employees receive training and are aware of the organizational policies for contractor access to sensitive information, classified systems, and materials.

15. Government employees should be instructed not to discuss sensitive information, classified material, or procurement data in areas where uncleared contractor personnel work. Government employees must be aware of their surroundings and avoid leaving sensitive information in open storage where contractor personnel may observe it. They must also ensure that proprietary information is not released to contractor personnel without a legitimate need to know based on the requirements of the contract.

16. Ensure that contractors are restricted from accessing proprietary-acquisition information, contract-proposal data, bid information, contractor performance reviews, or internal government communications relating to acquisition planning and determinations.

17. Ensure that contractor personnel receive similar training as their government counterparts on issues of counterintelligence threat and industrial espionage as they pertain to the areas of their work.

18. Avoid placing contractor personnel in positions of control over classified property or materials for which they have no legal accountability. Even if a contractor employee has authorization to review such material, they should not exercise primary responsibility for controlling, transporting, or securing this information outside of the government workspaces, unless specifically authorized by the terms of the contract or government supervisor.

19. Contractors should not be given responsibilities for facility security procedures unless this is the express purpose of their contract, such as in the case of contract security guards. This includes tasks such as key control, unsupervised presence in secure workspaces, or performing end-of-day facility security checks. These duties and responsibilities should be handled by appropriate government personnel and never delegated to contractor employees.

7

Supervisor Best Practices

THIS CHAPTER INTRODUCES a series of topics designed to help the supervisor manage operations of the blended government-contractor workforce. The tips and recommendations focus on common mistakes that tend to occur in mixed workplaces. The good news for supervisors is that most of these oversights can be boiled down to a handful of key problem areas primarily relating to organizational conflict of interest, procurement-integrity violations, and inadequate oversight and surveillance of contractor performance. Many of these problems are easily avoided by adhering to a few basic rules of thumb, perhaps the most important of which is providing adequate workforce training to educate government employees on their responsibilities and implementing necessary safeguards in the workplace. If the supervisor can concentrate on avoiding problems in these key areas it is likely that the commercial partnership will be successful and conducted in a manner that is efficient, productive, and ethical.

The list below summarizes a few of the more commonly observed problems that arise on mixed government-contractor teams. Supervisors should be aware of these issues and be proactive against their occurrence in the workplace.

Commonly Observed Problems in the Blended Workforce

- improper use of personal-services contracts
- contractor performance of out-of-scope activities
- misapplication of federal supply schedules for unauthorized services

- inadequate contract surveillance
- poor contract-administration procedures
- unsatisfactory evaluation and oversight of contractor work
- contractor performance of inherently governmental functions
- government personnel improperly seeking contractor employment
- contractor misuse of government property
- misuse or unauthorized disclosure of sensitive procurement information
- organizational conflict of interest
- contractor security violations
- improper modification to task orders, requirements, and contract scope of work

Many frequently observed errors are related to just a few reoccurring challenges for supervisors and government employees. Perhaps the most endemic problem in the government-contractor workforce is the frequency of personal-services violations. This problem is often an indicator of other concerns, since these types of errors reflect related issues of inadequate government supervision and mismanagement of contractor employees.

It is a commonly heard refrain these days that it is nearly impossible to distinguish government employees from contractor personnel. This is due in part to the ubiquity of contractor personnel in the government workplace but also to the fact that many contractor functions are nearly indistinguishable from the activities performed by the government personnel sitting next to them. Nevertheless, this situation is often an indicator of other potential problems in the government workplace. If an outside observer walks into a government office and cannot immediately distinguish the contractor from a government worker, either by nature of their duties or by overt identification, this is a clear sign that a workplace may have deficiencies in oversight and management controls.

One of the most common errors of inexperienced government managers is the tendency to treat contractor employees exactly like government workers. This error may inadvertently lead to a host of other problems, including contractors performing inherently governmental functions and out-of-scope activities, committing personal-services violations, modifying contract requirements without authorization, and communicating unauthorized commitments on behalf of the government.

Many of the problems cited in the list above arise from basic misperceptions concerning appropriate roles, responsibilities, and authorities of government versus contractor personnel. When supervisors and employees do not respect and reinforce the distinctions between government and contractor personnel, mistakes and violations become inevitable.

Avoiding Organizational Conflict of Interest Problems

During the course of normal duties, supervisors are exposed to significant amounts of information concerning government requirements, requests for proposal, solicitation plans, and other procurement-sensitive data. This type of information often becomes the source of potential conflict-of-interest concerns in the government-contractor workplace. Issues arise from the intentional or inadvertent disclosure of information relating to such matters as contractor bids, proposal information, source-selection data, vendor performance evaluations, or information on the award of future contracts. Supervisors must be aware of the potential risks of improper disclosure of this information during all interactions with contactor employees and vendor representatives.

In very general terms, organizational conflict of interest may be understood as situations in which the nature of work performed under a proposed or current government contract results in an unfair competitive advantage to the contractor or impairs the contractor's objectivity in performance of their work. Beyond this, acquisition regulations are not entirely specific about defining conflict of interest or identifying situations in which it is likely to occur. The FAR explains that "each individual contracting situation should be examined on the basis of its particular facts and the nature of the proposed contract. The exercise of common sense, good judgment, and sound discretion is required in both the decision on whether a significant potential conflict exists and, if it does, the development of an appropriate means for resolving it."[1]

The FAR goes on to describe two underlying principles that define the government's goals with regard to conflict of interest problems:

- to prevent the existence of conflicting roles that might bias a contractor's judgment
- to prevent unfair competitive advantage

As the FAR passage suggests, much of the determination comes down to supervisors acting responsibly and applying common sense in their dealings with vendors and contractor employees. Supervisors should be aware of the potential for these problems to occur in the workplace and make every effort to educate their employees about potentially risky situations. Furthermore, supervisors should draw on the knowledge and experience of the COR, contracting officer, and organizational legal advisor when questions arise concerning possible conflicts of interest in their workplace.

The list below offers a few questions that the supervisor should consider to help identify possible scenarios in which conflicts of interest may arise in their workplace.[2]

- Do potential bidders perform work in such a way as to permit them to devise solutions or make recommendations that could influence the award of future contracts?
- Are potential bidders involved in developing system-design specifications that could influence the outcome of current or future contracts?
- Have potential bidders participated in earlier work involving the same program or activity that is the subject of a current contract proposal?
- Did any bidders on a contract have previous access to source selection or proprietary information not available to other bidders competing for the work?
- Will a contractor be evaluating a competitor's work?
- Does the contract allow the vendor to accept its own products or activities on behalf of the government?
- Is the contractor in any way responsible for evaluating or documenting the government's record of their performance?
- Will the work under contract put the contractor in a position to influence government decision making such as developing regulations that will affect the vendor's current or future business?
- Will the work under this contract affect the interests of the contractor's other clients?
- Are any potential bidders, or personnel performing on the contract, former agency officials who personally and substantially participated in the development of the requirement and procurement of these services within the past two years?

Tips for Avoiding Potential Conflicts of Interest

Although government supervisors do not have any direct role in the contract-proposal and bidding process, their proximity to government operations and knowledge of contact requirements makes them privy to sensitive information that should not be discussed with contractors, vendor representatives, or bidders on new government requirements. Due to their position and access to sensitive information, supervisors must be continually aware of potentially improper inquiries from contractor employees, vendors, and potential bidders for government contracts.

The tips below provide a general overview of some issues of concern to help the supervisor monitor their workplace for potential problems. It is always best to consult with the COR or contracting officer for specific information on possible conflict-of-interest violations or questions involving sensitive discussions with contractor employees, vendors, or potential bidders.

1. Contractors must always be clearly identified in the workplace by appropriate badges, office designation, or clearly displayed markings denoting them as contractor employees. In all circumstances, whether in face-to-face interactions or via other written or verbal communication, the status of contractor employees must be clear to anyone interacting with them in an official capacity. This will help to avoid the inadvertent sharing of sensitive procurement or proprietary information.

2. Contractors with access to government e-mail must have user identifications or signature blocks that clearly indicate their status as company employees rather than government personnel. Contractors should always identify themselves as contractor employees when answering the phone and on voice mail or in any other verbal or written communication. This includes all signed memoranda, faxes, e-mails, and business cards.

3. Supervisors must provide appropriate workspace layout in order to ensure that there is no inadvertent disclosure of proprietary or sensitive information to nongovernment personnel. Contractors should be isolated from government workspaces where significant amounts of procurement activity occur in order to prevent the inadvertent disclosure of sensitive information.

4. Government supervisors should be aware of the legal limitations and restrictions on the disclosure of procurement information to contract employees and vendors. Be particularly careful in any situation in which a contractor employee or vendor representative engages in discussions concerning future requirements, ongoing bids, or performance evaluations of particular vendors providing services to the government.

5. Supervisors should be aware of the general stipulations of the Procurement Integrity Act. This act prohibits the release of source selection and contractor-bid or proposal information. It also restricts some activities of former government employees who served in positions relating to procurement actions or contracting, barring them from compensation as an employee or consultant of that contractor for a set period of time. The act also covers rules regarding government officials accepting other compensation from contractors as well as guidelines concerning disclosure of insider information relating to present and future government-acquisition plans.

6. Supervisors must exercise appropriate control over information relating to ongoing contracts. This includes such information as draft statements

of work, contractor performance evaluations, and other information that could potentially jeopardize the integrity of the procurement process or offer unfair advantage to a particular vendor or bidder in future contract negotiations.

7. During interactions with contractor employees or vendor representatives, supervisors and government employees must be sure to keep discussions focused on matters strictly limited to the execution of the current contract and not discuss contract options, renewal actions, rebids, or proposed modifications to the contract requirements.

8. Beware of making unauthorized commitments on behalf of the government. Any agreement made by a supervisor or COR is not legally binding. Only an authorized contracting officer can make commitments on behalf of the government. In dealings with vendor representatives, be cautious of offering suggestions, critiques, or modifications to requirements or any other promises relating to future work. Only the contracting officer is authorized to engage in such discussions with a vendor.

9. Do not assign contractors to teams with responsibility for making program decisions or providing major input to acquisition plans that would provide unfair advantage in future bids or competitions on those projects.

10. Under no circumstances should nonacquisition government supervisors engage in discussions with the vendor or contractor employees concerning expenditures of government funds, payments, and obligations. This authority is limited to the contracting officer or designated contract-obligation authority.

11. Supervisors and government employees must be aware of perceptions involving the receipt of gifts, rides, meals, or any form of compensation from a contractor employee or vendor. Such items may be construed as lending special access or favoritism toward a particular contract employee or vendor. Be sure to consult the COR or organizational ethics advisor for specific questions concerning monetary limits and appropriate circumstances in which a supervisor may accept gifts or minor services from a contractor or vendor representative. When in doubt about the legality or propriety of any transaction, make a written record of the incident in a memorandum for record and consult with the COR or organizational legal advisor.

12. Supervisors should not engage in discussions with contractor employees or vendor representatives concerning advance procurement information, contractor-performance data, future government requirements, pending requests for proposal, source-selection information, award

decisions, or other proprietary information relating to government-acquisition planning. Government employees are expressly prohibited from knowingly disclosing procurement information relating to their organization before the award of a contract.

13. Be aware of contacts with former government employees who have entered the private sector and now represent vendor interests. Supervisors should exercise extreme caution when engaging in discussions about procurement planning or the government's operational requirements with former employees who may possess familiarity with a particular support contract or an ongoing bidding process.

14. Be aware of circumstances in which a vendor presents unsolicited proposals or offers demonstrations of a product or service for consideration. Do not furnish unauthorized government resources, supplies, and office space or government time in support of such demonstrations. Any such offer must receive prior approval by the authorized contracting authority.

15. Be cognizant of unsolicited advice, recommendations, or referrals offered by a vendor. Be aware of possible perceptions of bias or special consideration expected in return for advice or referrals that are offered. Avoid any action or statement that gives the presumption of quid pro quo for unsolicited information or services provided by a vendor or their representatives.

16. Supervisors must maintain clear impartiality in all discussions with contractor employees and vendor representatives. As a supervisor, do not engage in discussions with a contractor or vendor representative relating to contract renewals and extension or express preference for one vendor's services over another.

17. Do not allow contractors to provide technical advice or conduct market research or source-selection activities relating to competing vendors or companies in which they have a vested interest.

18. Do not assign contractor employees to positions where they have responsibility for conducting performance evaluations or technical inspections on the work of their company or the work of other contractors.

19. Generally speaking, government supervisors are prohibited from endorsing any product or service provided by a vendor. Be extremely cautious when offering endorsements or personal recommendations for contractor employees relating to their work for a vendor on a government project. In most cases, it is advisable for government supervisors not to use their official title or government letterhead to make such endorsements or to provide personal letters of recommendations for former contractor employees. Always consult the organizational

ethics advisor for questions concerning appropriate actions in dealing with requests for recommendations or offering individual performance evaluations relating to a contractor employee's service in the government workplace.

20. Contracting officials or government supervisors are required to report any offers of future employment made by a vendor performing on a contract in which they have supervisory or administrative responsibility.

21. Generally speaking, a government supervisor should not work on a project with contractor partners if he or she has personal financial interests with the vendor, such as a spouse seeking employment with the contractor or significant stockholdings with the firm.

22. Ethics regulations prohibit a government supervisor from participating in outside employment with a contractor with which they have official duties and interactions. This general rule also applies to any other activity that may give the appearance of a government supervisor using their association with the vendor for personal gain.

23. Government supervisors should immediately consult the organizational ethics or legal advisor if they choose to quit government service and seek employment with a contractor working on projects related to the government supervisor's official duties. As a general rule of thumb, government supervisors should never work on government matters involving contractors with whom they are seeking employment.

24. Be aware that there are certain legal and ethical restrictions that apply to postgovernment employment with contractors. This includes bans on representing a vendor working on the same project on which the government supervisor worked during their time with the government. Consult the organizational legal advisor for specific guidelines and restrictions.

25. Certain conflict-of-interest rules apply for newly hired government employees limiting their association with contracts of their former employer. This is particularly true in cases where a new government supervisor may have significant continuing financial interests in a company, such as stock options.

Recognizing Inherently Governmental Functions

The issue of inherently governmental functions has gained significant attention in recent years as the massive expansion of federal-service contracting has placed contractors in much closer proximity to the execution of core governmental functions. In order to satisfy government mission requirements while adhering to mandated hiring ceilings, some agencies are now using contractors for functions previously done only by civil servants. Additionally, a recent study by the Acquisition Advisory Panel found that much of the current expansion of federal-service contracting has occurred outside of the discipline of OMB Circular A-76 procedures.[3] This has resulted in unclear definitions and inconsistent application of guidance pertaining to inherently governmental functions.

To a significant degree, the promotion of concepts like blended workforce have only made the distinctions more difficult to recognize and enforce, particularly in environments where contractors work side-by-side with their government counterparts on substantively similar functions. This situation inevitably blurs boundaries, influences the decision-making process, and compromises the integrity of the government-contractor relationship.

In a perfect world this would not be an issue of concern for a government supervisor. Clear contract language, workplace safeguards, and active supervision by the COR would all provide ample protections against contractors inadvertently performing functions considered inherently governmental. Yet the reality today in many government workplaces is that collaboration between government and contractor employees is almost seamless, and in many situations the functions performed are nearly indistinguishable. This reality makes it necessary for government supervisors to be informed about the basic rules concerning inherently governmental functions and aware of potential violations occurring in their workplace.

Close cooperation between government and contractor employees often blurs the nature of the contributions from each side, sometimes making it difficult for an uninformed observer to easily discern where the contractor's contribution ends and government authority begins. It is in this ambiguous zone of interface where the government supervisor must exercise extreme caution to ensure that contractors do not slip beyond the scope of their assigned tasks and authorities and engage in work that is considered inherently governmental. This is particularly important in cases where contractor employees are working in close support of military, intelligence, or law-enforcement operations, where their contributions must be clearly circumscribed and distinguishable in order to maintain the integrity of government authority and responsibility.

Because the COR will not always be present to serve as a safeguard and monitor of contractor work, the government supervisor possess a basic understanding of inherently governmental functions and must be able to recognize when contractor employees are engaging in work that is beyond the scope of their authorities. The Federal Acquisition Regulation (FAR) should be consulted for explicit descriptions of inherently governmental activities as established by the Office of Federal Procurement Policy. As a general rule contractors should not perform tasks or services directly related to the integral effort of an agency's core functions. Nor should contractors take part, either directly or indirectly, in tasks requiring the direction or supervision of government personnel in order to protect the government's interest.

Since there is a significant level of ambiguity in the FAR guidelines, typically each agency is responsible for determining whether specific functions and tasks within their purview are inherently governmental and providing contracting officials with written determinations on applicable restrictions.

The list below offers some general guidance on identifying inherently governmental functions but should not be used by a government supervisor for making independent determinations on specific tasks or activities performed by contractors in their workplace. In any case where a government supervisor has concerns over a specific activity performed by a contractor employee, the COR should be immediately consulted for advice and assistance.

Inherently Governmental Functions[4]

- direct conduct of criminal investigations
- command of military forces or military members serving in combat, combat support, or combat-service support roles
- conduct of foreign relations or determination of foreign policy
- determination of government-agency policies or regulations
- determination of federal-program priorities for budget requests
- direction, control, and supervision of federal employees
- direction and control of intelligence and counterintelligence operations
- hiring determinations for federal-government employment
- approval of job descriptions and performance standards for federal employees
- preparation of, or approval authority for, responses to Freedom of Information Act requests
- determination on adjudication of security clearances
- approval of federal-licensing actions and inspections
- determination of budget policy, guidance, and strategy
- collection, control, and disbursement of certain fees, royalties, duties, fines, taxes, and other public funds
- control of the treasury accounts and administration of public trusts
- drafting of congressional testimony, responses to congressional correspondence
- preparation of agency responses to audit reports from government inspectors

Avoiding Personal-Services and Scope-of-Work Violations

Two of the most common mistakes made by government supervisors are the improper use of personal services and scope-of-work violations. This problem arises from the natural tendency for inexperienced supervisors to treat contractor employees as they would a government subordinate, thus creating the potential for violations of FAR guidelines against personal-services contracts. A service contract may be either personal or nonpersonal in nature. In general, personal services are those contracted activities that, by terms of the contract or by conduct of administration, give the appearance of the contractor being a government employee. Except for certain specific circumstances outlined in the Federal Acquisition Regulation, the government generally only contracts for nonpersonal services. In simple terms, this means that the government cannot hire contractors to be used in the same manner as a government employee, nor can supervisors exercise similar control and management authority over contractor personnel as they may a government worker.

The basic concept to remember for avoiding potential personal-services violations is that supervisors should manage process, not people, when it comes to their interactions with the contractor workforce. Government supervisors are there to manage government operations. Contractor service augments and supports these operations, but the supervisor must remember to avoid any conduct or action that might suggest the existence of an employer-employee relationship with contractor personnel.

When in doubt, the litmus-test question supervisors should ask is, "Does the performance of the contractor's assigned tasks require the exercise of continuous supervision, control, and direction on the part of the government supervisor?" If the answer to this question is yes, then there is a clear risk that the tasks being performed by the contractor imply an employer-employee relationship, representing a possible personal-services violation. Furthermore, there is a good chance that the performance of these tasks may also reside outside the permissible scope of work outlined in the contract language.

Scope of work violations often go hand in hand with personal services violations due to the fact that when a supervisor makes the error of treating the contractor like a government employee, they often do so within the context of requesting the performance of services or duties falling outside the contract statement of work. Fortunately, both errors are easily avoided by adhering to a few basic rules of thumb to ensure that an appropriate government-contractor relationship is maintained.

A list of warning signs is provided below to help alert supervisors to possible situations in which personal-services violations are likely to occur in the workplace. In many cases there is a fine line between appropriate and inappropriate use of contractor support. Supervisors are encouraged to consult with the COR or organizational legal advisor if uncertain about specific cases in the workplace.

General Factors Indicating Potential Personal-Services Contracts

- performance of work on site at a government office, installation, or facility
- use of tools and equipment furnished by the government
- services applied directly to the integral effort of an agency or organization
- comparable services performed in other agencies using civil service personnel
- need for service provided can reasonably be expected to last beyond one year
- inherent nature of service, or manner in which it is provided, reasonably requires government direction or supervision of contractor employees in order to protect government interest or retain control of the function involved
- nature of work places a contractor in position of command, supervision, administration, or control over government personnel or the personnel of other contractors
- performance of duties gives the appearance that contractor is part of government organization

Tips for Avoiding Personal-Services Violations

1. Avoid any circumstances or interactions that give the appearance of an employer-employee relationship.
2. Do not use government and contractor personnel interchangeably.
3. Supervisors should not direct the activities of contractor employees or exercise supervisory authority over them. Only the COR has authority to direct performance of contractor employees through direction of the vendor's site manager.
4. Always ensure that the vendor's manager, rather than government personnel, is assigning tasks and providing supervisory direction to contractor personnel.
5. CORs and supervisors should ensure that the tasks assigned to contractor employees are clearly defined so that day-to-day direction and supervision by a government employee is not required.

6. Supervisors must ensure that the assignment of any tasks not clearly specified in the contract language is cleared through the COR or CO before the contractor begins work in order to avoid potential scope-of-work violations for which the government may be liable.

7. As a general rule of thumb, government supervisors should keep in mind the following restrictions when dealing with contractor employees:

   - Do not exercise direct managerial control over issues such as work hours, vacation, sick leave, time cards, duty rosters, or other administrative concerns as you would for government employees.
   - Do not administer or direct the training of contractor personnel.
   - Do not conduct individual performance appraisals, counseling, or evaluations for contractor personnel.
   - Do not apply disciplinary measures to contractor personnel or approve awards, bonuses, special recognitions, or incentives.
   - Do not become involved in the selection, hiring, recruiting, or firing of contractor personnel. Do not direct a site manager or other vendor representative to hire or fire particular contractor employees.
   - Do not become involved in any discussions with contractor employees regarding assignments, pay issues, performance bonuses, or programmed incentives.

8. Do not place contractors in any position that requires them to exercise personal judgment or discretion on behalf of the government.

9. Do not exercise more than limited technical authority or control over contractor personnel in the performance of their daily duties. Contractor employees do not report directly to government employees for tasking, direction, or guidance on the performance of daily functions.

10. Do not permit contractors to exercise command, supervisory, or managerial control over government employees or perform inherently governmental functions.

11. Government supervisors cannot authorize compensatory time for contractor employees, approve early release from work or overtime pay, or request assistance from contractor employees in organizing office activities or social functions not directly stipulated in the terms of the contract.

12. Supervisors must ensure that changes to instructions, work schedules, or modifications to the workflow process are approved by the COR and implemented through the vendor's site manager.

13. Supervisors must ensure that contractor employees are not listed in organizational charts or chain-of-command diagrams depicting them as an organic part of the government's staff. Their designation

as contractor should be clearly indicated on all official organizational information and charts.

14. Government supervisors cannot approve requests for contractor employees to attend government-sponsored training unless specifically stipulated in the contract or cleared through the COR and contracting officer.

15. Government supervisors will not take part in interviewing contractor employees for specific job functions or assignments, nor should they recommend individual contractor employees for specific jobs, positions, or tasks. The vendor's management team makes these determinations.

16. Government supervisors should not assign or delegate tasks to specific contractor employees or make decisions concerning employee workloads of the vendor's team.

17. Although the supervisor should make every effort to provide a safe and enjoyable workplace for all employees, it is important to remember that ultimate responsibility for the morale, health, and welfare of contractor employees resides with the vendor's management team, not with the government supervisor.

Notes

1. FAR, subpart 9.5, *Organizational and Consultant Conflicts of Interest.*

2. The checklist is derived from the Office of Federal Procurement Policy (OFPP), policy letter 93-1, *Management Oversight of Service Contracting.*

3. *Report of the Acquisition Advisory Panel,* Office of Federal Procurement Policy and the United States Congress, January 2007, 24.

4. See FAR, subpart 7.5, *Inherently Governmental Functions.*

8

Evaluating Contractor Performance

PERHAPS THE MOST SIGNIFICANT CONTRIBUTION that the government supervisor provides to the acquisition team is assistance in developing and facilitating a workable plan for evaluating contractor performance. A basic rule of thumb is that the government should never hire contractors to do work that cannot be effectively measured, monitored, and quantified. Absence of clear measuring sticks for evaluating contractor output invariably results in problems with the partnership and waste of government resources. If the acquisition team and supervisor do not have a clear picture of what success should look like and how it will be measured, then there is little chance that the endeavor will yield positive results for the government.

It is important to remember that the primary responsibility for measuring, monitoring, and evaluating contractor performance falls to the contracting officer and the COR. Nevertheless, in many government workplaces the supervisor will play a critical role facilitating and assisting in the monitoring and evaluation of contractor performance. Supervisors are most likely to have continual day-to-day interaction with the contractor at the site of performance and, hence, will frequently have the best understanding of the contractor's overall performance of any member of the acquisition team. For this reason supervisors must have a clear understanding of how contract surveillance and evaluation are conducted and how they can help the acquisition team with the process.

Establishing a Surveillance Methodology

It is important that both the acquisition team and the supervisor have a clear and mutual understanding of the surveillance methodology. This ensures that the right kind of information will be gathered to enable an accurate and complete assessment of the contractor's performance. This is important not only to ensure that the contractor is providing services that satisfy the terms of the contract but also to establish a solid record of past performance that may be used as a reference when the contractor bids on future government work. It is the obligation of the acquisition team, with the help of the supervisor, to ensure that this happens.

As the acquisition team begins the process of developing the surveillance methodology, there are some basic questions that should be considered to ensure that the right kind of data is collected and the contractor's performance effectively measured. Supervisors and acquisition specialists should ask the following questions as they begin developing a surveillance methodology.

1. What is the end-state product or service that the contractor is being asked to provide, and how is successful delivery defined?
2. What are the required standards of quality?
3. What are the measures indicating that this standard has been achieved?
4. How will output and process efficiency be measured?
5. What type of measurements will be used?
6. How frequently will measurements occur?
7. What statistics, tools, or data-sampling procedures are required to make the assessment?
8. Who will collect the data?
9. How will the information be documented and reported?

One important thing to consider when developing an effective surveillance methodology is how to determine the best method for capturing a complete snapshot of the contractor's performance. This may require a mix of sampling techniques, including both quantitative and qualitative measures.

The task of determining what elements of contractor performance to assess can be complicated for service-based contracts. Oftentimes, measuring the results of a contractor's activities can be ambiguous when a service does not have a well-defined end state or analogous commercial standard. Evaluating the quality of services is generally much more difficult than evaluating delivery of tangible product, which lends itself to clear technical specifications and production standards. This is particularly true if the contractor's output is conceptual in nature, such as investigations, analytical reports, evaluations, process studies, or research and development projects.

Generally speaking, there are three types of basic measures that may be applied to evaluation of a contractor's performance.

- *Measures of economy.* Does the contractor provide the appropriate quantity of a good or service at the best price?
- *Measures of efficiency.* Does the contractor make the best use of available resources in terms of labor hours, materials, costs, and process?
- *Measures of effectiveness.* Does the contractor accomplish the basic objective or task? Are customers and users satisfied with the outcome of the contractor's service? Are all measures of quality and timeliness satisfied?

Enabling Effective Contract Surveillance

Once the acquisition team has determined a basic methodology for measuring contractor performance, they can begin developing the step-by-step process for the surveillance program. A surveillance program is nothing more than the application of a systematic methodology for monitoring, measuring, collecting, and documenting data on a contractor's performance. A complete plan should also include procedures for identifying and resolving contractor performance deficiencies, as well as steps for ensuring corrective action.

In all cases the COR and contracting officer will be the lead agents in this process, but, depending on the nature of the contract and circumstances of work, the supervisor may play a significant role in developing and implementing certain aspects of the surveillance plan. At the very least, the COR will require close cooperation and involvement by the government supervisor in order to facilitate the inspection program so that the day-to-day performance of the contractor is adequately measured, assessed, and reported.

The tips below offer some general guidelines and recommendations to consider during the process of developing and implementing an effective contract-surveillance plan.

1. *Focus the surveillance methodology on output-centered evaluation.* There is a natural tendency for government supervisors to focus too much on the contractor's internal processes at the expense of measuring outputs. The government supervisor's role is not to manage the contractor's process; this is the function of the vendor's management team. Rather, the supervisor's role is to oversee the government's workflow process

and to design an efficient system so that the contractor is free to do their work and deliver the required goods or services. To facilitate this process, the government team should establish an acceptable quality level (AQL), defining the baseline standards of delivery, and then provide the vendor's site manager with the maximum possible latitude to develop optimal solutions for how his or her team can best achieve that standard. The COR and the supervisor's roles should focus on developing and implementing a surveillance plan focused on measuring and evaluating the output of that process.

2. *Have a standardized approach for assessing performance.* The standards used for assessing a contractor's performance will vary significantly depending on the type of contract and nature of the services being delivered. It is important that the evaluation methodology not be excessively cumbersome to implement, manage, or sustain. No single methodology is applicable for every type of contract or process, but effective assessment systems will all share some common characteristics.

- They must have clear definitions of what is being measured.
- They must be developed in accordance with contract terms and requirements.
- They should have well-defined quantitative and qualitative criteria.
- Measurements and data collection methodologies should be statistically based whenever possible.
- Criteria should be focused on output more than process.
- Evaluation methodology must be transparent, unbiased, and objective.
- Data-collection procedures should be efficient, unobtrusive, and minimally disruptive to the contractor's work.
- The inspection regimen should not demand an excessive number of government personnel and time to implement or maintain.
- Inspections should be consistent in type, scope, and procedure.
- Measurements and data should be standardized and easily gathered.
- Measurements and evaluations should employ recognized commercial standards whenever possible.
- If possible, the assessment methodology should remain consistent throughout the life of the contract to maintain the integrity of the data.
- Government evaluations should integrate vendor self-assessments whenever possible.

3. *Develop clear criteria for measuring contractor performance.* Once the acquisition team has developed a good description of the services to be

delivered, they must then establish specific criteria for what aspects of the contractor's performance will be measured and how these measurements will be assessed. Criteria will vary significantly from contract to contract depending on the type of service. Generally speaking, it is much more difficult to design an assessment program for services than tangible items where delivery standards are based on highly specified technical measures. The evaluation of services can be ambiguous, particularly when the product is conceptual in nature, such as analysis, process development, scientific research, report writing, and administrative or staff-support functions. This challenge is even more difficult when the government's requirement does not have a clearly analogous commercial standard. Nevertheless, it is critical that the government develop objective statistical measures for evaluating contractor performance whenever possible.

Selected performance measures should provide the COR and supervisor with a series of qualitative and quantitative indicators to determine whether the vendor's performance is satisfactory and cost effective to the government. Performance may be evaluated using a variety of statistical and technical measures depending on the nature of the service being delivered. Some examples of qualitative measures include workload figures, output-to-cost ratios, transaction ratios, error rates, consumption rates, inventory-fill rates, labor-hour efficiency measures, production timelines, and completion schedules. Measures of quality in services may include such data as responsiveness rates, user-satisfaction rates, customer-feedback surveys, production-quality measures, outcome analysis, and adherence to standards expressed in the statement of objectives.

The list below provides a few examples of general qualitative measures that may be considered as possible assessment criteria for evaluating contractor services. While this list is not exhaustive, it does provide some basic ideas about how to approach the problem of developing assessment criteria for service-based contracting.

- Contractor response time on task requests.
- Adherence to delivery deadlines or performance schedules.
- Error and accuracy rates—This measure can be based on the number of mistakes or errors in the delivery of a product as well as services. This process can be used for developing statistical measures for the number of revisions required in submission of contractor work based on established quality standards. Standard deviations of performance trends may be applied to determine a range of acceptable quality.

- Milestone completion—Major projects may have interim-performance milestones or phased-delivery goals used to gauge progress during a long-term effort.
- Cost controls—If the work is based on a cost-reimbursement or cost-plus contract there may be certain criteria established to measure the contractor's success in controlling costs within an estimated range or target.
- Adherence to relevant government regulations, technical measures, or production quality standards.
- Rate of days free from safety incidents or security violations.
- Use of efficient business practices in the contractor's internal process.
- Contractor application of effective management techniques or cost-savings initiatives.
- Introduction of contractor-led process solutions or use of innovation for greater efficiency.
- Receipt of customer-feedback or -satisfaction surveys from end users of the contractor's goods or services.
- Receipt of quality awards or recognition for outstanding performance by customers or outside auditors.
- Effective management of contractor personnel, including minimizing personnel turnover, increasing retention, improving process efficiency through minimizing personnel retraining requirements, lowering transition, and training time for new contractor personnel.

4. *Develop a quality-assurance plan.* Contracts should always have a written quality-assurance plan (also referred to as a quality-assurance-surveillance plan) clearly outlining how the surveillance methodology will be applied. This plan should address the specific steps that the COR or other technical monitors will use to assess the contractor's performance against standards outlined in the statement of work.

   The quality-assurance plan should be sufficiently detailed to identify all critical elements for effective implementation of the surveillance program, including a list of performance indicators, quality standards, inspection methods, and procedures used for gathering, documenting, and reporting performance data. The plan should focus on evaluating the end-state product or service rather than focusing on the actual process used by the contractor.

   The quality-assurance plan should be simple enough that it can be easily implemented and sustained with minimal burden to the government. It should include specified procedures for data collection, methods of surveillance, thresholds for acceptable and unacceptable performance, sampling procedures, and examples of formats for reporting and documentation.

All quality-assurance plans must, at the very least, include the following basic elements:

- statement of purpose
- list of what will be monitored
- procedures for how monitoring will take place
- assignment of who will conduct the monitoring
- description of how the results will be documented
- procedures for remediation of observed deficiencies

5. *Develop the inspection regimen.* There are a variety of ways in which the acquisition team can approach the process of data collection. Surveillance plans and data-collection processes will vary greatly from situation to situation. It is important that supervisors work closely with the COR and contracting officer to determine the most effective sampling methodology for gathering the required information. It is important that the inspection regimen not be excessively burdensome for the government to implement or significantly interfere with the contractor's work. The regimen must be consistent in methodology, process, and scope. If the standards or criteria for measurement continually change during the course of the contract, the data set will be useless for evaluating contractor performance.

Once the assessment criteria and methodology have been developed, the acquisition team must next determine the appropriate frequency and type of inspection. For example, a program may be based on 100 percent, periodic, or random sampling. This choice is dependent on the nature of the product or service being provided, contract type, location of work, manner of performance, and size and flexibility of the government's surveillance team. There is no single-best system for every contract. Below is a basic description of the general sampling types that might be used.

- *100 percent inspection.* This method evaluates all outputs produced by the contractor. It is most applicable to small quantities of production or services in which government supervisors or quality-assurance inspectors can devote significant time and resources to monitoring production-quality standards. Because of the time and resources involved in this type of inspection regime, it is not a desirable or appropriate method for most contractor inspections. Nevertheless, it may be used in situations where the deliverables must meet stringent government requirements, such as tasks involving law-enforcement investigations, public-safety matters, intelligence operations, or security services.

- *Random sampling.* This methodology is a statistically grounded approach based on the assumption that a randomly selected survey of contractor work will reflect a valid picture of overall performance. This method will require some investment of time and effort in validating data samples to ensure that the sample size and frequency of inspections provide statistically sound results. This system generally works best in situations where large amounts of the contractor's output can be easily gathered and analyzed for trends and deficiencies. It is best for measuring tasks that are frequently performed and highly standardized.

- *Periodic sampling or fixed sampling.* This method is a variation of random sampling, based on a snapshot of the contractor's performance taken at set times or phase-based intervals. This method is nothing more than a fixed inspection schedule set at planned intervals or dates. It is useful for situations in which the nature of the contractor's work is routine and longitudinal performance data may be easily gathered and reviewed at fixed intervals. One advantage of this method is that it minimizes the amount of time that the COR or government supervisor must devote to measuring and assessing contractor performance, since it does not require continuous oversight and evaluation. Periodicity may be based on fixed inspections times, major project milestones, phases of the contract's option cycle, or even the discretion of the COR based on other queuing performance indicators. This methodology is less taxing than 100 percent inspections but offers a less telling assessment of contractor performance than true random sampling. Since periodic sampling may be influenced by other factors, it may not provide a statistically valid representation of a contractor's total effort and performance.

6. *Integrating other performance assessment tools.* Below are a few examples of other methodologies that can be applied to gather contractor performance information. These techniques may not be used as the primary assessment methodology but can offer useful supplementary performance data for developing a holistic assessment of a contractor's performance.

   - *Use of contractor internal assessments.* This may include government reviews of contractor-maintained quality-assurance data. Site managers should have this type of data as part of their internal quality-assurance plan. Some contractors may use automated management-information systems to maintain certain types of performance data, including production rates, efficiency, quality control rates, and labor-productivity measures. Due to conflict-of-interest concerns, review of the contractor's own internal performance assessments should not be the sole means of conducting evaluation but may be integrated as part of the government's overall surveillance plan.

- *Trend analysis.* This methodology is really nothing more than the continual collection of contractor-performance metrics and the analysis of changing patterns of production output. This methodology is particularly useful for habitual processes with standardized, predictable levels of output and with services that lend themselves to long-term data collection. This method requires the use of database tools and the ability to easily collect and input daily performance data. An advantage of this methodology is that it can provide very detailed statistical information on contractor efficiency and help supervisors make accurate assessments about how certain changes in procedures, resource inputs, and workflow process can affect contractor performance. Another benefit from this method is that the government can use the contractor's own metrics from their quality control plan to populate the database and analyze results.

- *Customer feedback and satisfaction surveys.* If the government is providing a product or service to outside customers—either taxpayers or other government agencies—it may be useful to consider integrating this feedback into the overall assessment of the contractor's performance. This technique requires consideration of how external feedback may be gathered, standardized, and quantified. It is important to establish a standardized methodology for sampling procedures and formatting in order to make this data as objective and formalized as possible. This may require the development of customer-feedback forms or satisfaction surveys provided to end users. The gathered information must also be validated just like any other assessment methodology to ensure consistency and accuracy of response data. Supervisors must also be aware of the inherent bias of customer-feedback systems, since service complaints are generally returned more frequently than positive evaluations. For this reason, customer feedback should not be the only performance metric for contractor evaluation. Nevertheless, it can provide a useful external check and balance to supplement other internal assessment methods.

- *External audits.* External evaluations and third-party audits may be used to draw on the expertise and objectivity of an independent, outside observer. Both the government and the contractor should agree to this technique, and the program should be clearly described in the contract language. The advantage of using this methodology is that it presents an opportunity for an external observer to assess the entirety of the operation, including analysis of the government's workflow process and operations. This type of objective, holistic assessment is difficult to achieve if only the government is conducting the performance review of the contractor's effort. There is a natural tendency for government inspectors to externalize problems and shift focus away from possible design flaws in the government's operations and look only for deficiencies in the contractor's performance. There are certainly many occasions where the poor performance of a contractor is due to failures of the government's internal management processes rather than problems with the contractor's own effort. An external audit provides an opportunity for an outside observer to critique the entire enterprise, offer objective review of the holistic process, and provide recommendations for improving the function of the overall government-contractor partnership.

- *Collaborative performance reviews.* This method is nothing more than a cooperative performance self-assessment where the government-contractor team conducts a partnered review examining the entire blended operation. This can be done as part of regularly scheduled inspections or simply as informal meetings between the supervisor, site manager, and COR. The benefit of such cooperative assessments is the opportunity they provide to leverage the knowledge and experience of both the government and contractor teams. This technique can lead to the development of collaborative solutions for addressing shared deficiencies and problems in the overall workflow process. It is a relatively rare occurrence when the root of a performance issue is only on one side of the government-contractor team. More often than not there is some degree of shared blame on each side when process deficiencies or performance problems are discovered. Applying the technique of collaborative review will help identify these collective areas of concern and promote the development of mutually beneficial solutions to optimize the function of the partnership.

Supervisor's Tips for Implementing the Surveillance Plan

Once the surveillance methodology has been developed, the next step is implementing the plan to collect and document the required performance data. No matter how good a quality-assurance plan is, unless the COR or technical monitors can effectively monitor performance and gather the required information, the plan is without value.

General methodology and processes for surveillance should be outlined in the contract, but detailed procedures and checklists will likely be developed by the contracting officer and the COR. The government supervisor can play an important role in this effort, assisting the COR in developing and executing the quality-assurance plan. The actual function of the performance-monitoring program will depend significantly on constraints imposed by the type of operation and availability of the COR or other technical monitors. Government supervisors can help facilitate this work by supplementing the effort of the COR with their own feedback and data on contractor performance.

There will be cases in which the COR is not be colocated at the site of performance. This is a less-than-ideal but not entirely uncommon occurrence. In such instances, the contracting officer may authorize the COR to delegate certain responsibilities for surveillance and data collection to the government supervisor or other appointed technical monitors. Even in cases in which the COR is in close proximity to the site of performance, the supervisor will still play a critical role in communicating observations and performance data back to the COR. Frequently the supervisor will possess a much more detailed picture of the technical processes and day-to-day operations of the contractor. For this reason, it is critically important that the supervisor be closely involved with the COR in the implementation of the surveillance plan. Supervisor feedback and input is absolutely necessary for keeping the acquisition team informed about progress of the contract.

The tips below provide some additional issues for consideration that will help the supervisor assist the COR and contracting officer in implementing an effective surveillance and monitoring program.

1. *Have a detailed quality-assurance-surveillance plan (QASP).* First and foremost, supervisors must ensure that the COR provides a written quality-assurance-surveillance plan, developed as part of the contract-administration process. This document should be the basis for the entire inspection regimen. It should contain a checklist of specific steps that the COR will use to perform surveillance and assess contractor performance. The quality-assurance-surveillance plan should be based on specifications taken directly from the contract statement of work. Ideally it should include detailed written instructions on inspection schedules and checklists, including all performance criteria and metrics that must be monitored. The plan should detail when inspections will occur, how they will be performed, what data will be collected, who will conduct the inspections, and how results will be documented and reported to the

contracting officer. The COR and the supervisor should work together to ensure that there are sufficient resources, time, and trained personnel to properly execute the plan.

2. *Establish a detail-focused inspection program.* The supervisor should work with the COR to determine the most effective process for implementing the inspection plan and the schedule for performance of surveillance activities. The supervisor must be closely involved in this process so that the inspection regimen is administered in a manner that is efficient and not disruptive to the overall operation of the government workplace. Below are a few issues to consider when developing the detailed inspection plan.

- Determine exactly how both announced and unannounced inspections will be administered. During this process, seek input from the vendor site manager to ensure that they are aware of the details of the inspection program and how it will be administered. The vendor's site manager should never be surprised by the scope or format of inspections, nor should inspections be designed to catch the vendor with a list of unexpected deficiencies. The purpose of the inspection is to ensure that delivery standards are achieved and to minimize potential for contractor error.

- Determine major project milestones and other logical review points that will be used to assess overall progress on the contract. In addition to regularly scheduled and unscheduled inspections, consider whether the nature of the project warrants establishing major periodic appraisals or reviews at certain critical junctures of the contract lifecycle.

- Determine which documents and records must be reviewed during each inspection period. This may include reviews of operational data maintained by the government supervisor, as well as documentation and records kept by the vendor site manager, such as daily logs, progress reports, or results of the vendor's internal quality-assurance inspections.

- Combine contractor inspections with periodic reviews of the government's workflow data and efficiency measures to ensure that both the contractor and the government's processes are analyzed holistically. This method will help government supervisors continually refine their workflow process and ensure that any observed deficiencies in contractor performance are not related to, or caused by, problems with government processes.

- Determine what tools or reference materials are required to properly execute the inspection program. Ensure that all required reference materials, sampling tools, technical manuals, checklists, and work-sheets are available for both the inspectors and the contractor team.

- Ensure that the COR or designated inspection representatives have all the necessary resources to properly execute the inspection program. This may include considerations for sufficient allocation of time, availability of measurement tools and reference materials, adequate proximity to the site of work, presence of key contractor personnel, or specialized training that may be required in order to perform inspection duties. The supervisor should ensure that these factors are taken into consideration so that inspection periods are minimally disruptive to contractor and government operations.
- Ensure that the vendor develops and implements an internal quality-control plan. This plan is intended to provide the vendor with a quality review mechanism and program controls over their internal process. The vendor's plan should describe the steps that they will take to identify and correct potential deficiencies in their output or process. Some requests for proposal will require that the vendor develop a plan for quality control as part of the bid proposal. In any case, the contacting officer should stipulate that the contractor develop and implement a written program for internal quality review. Elements of this plan may be referenced as part of the government's evaluative criteria used during periodic inspections.

3. *Determine the supervisor's responsibilities for implementing the surveillance plan.* Ensure that the surveillance plan clearly indicates who is responsible for all steps relating to inspection, gathering, and reporting of contractor performance data. In cases where it is difficult for the COR to continuously monitor performance, it may be appropriate to appoint quality-assurance evaluators or additional technical monitors to assist in gathering performance data. Distributed contractor operations or highly technical requirements may require enhanced monitoring techniques, special tools, or additional training for government evaluators. In such cases, the contracting officer and COR should appoint special quality-assurance monitors, technical inspectors, or COTRs as required. Below are some basic questions that the supervisor should ask to ensure that appropriate surveillance measures are present in their workplace.

- Who will conduct inspections and evaluations?
- Will the COR personally conduct all assessments?
- Will additional technical monitors or COTRs be appointed?

- What role will the supervisor or other government employees play in assisting with inspections or providing supplementary performance data?
- What is the schedule for inspections?
- What are the information requirements for inspections?
- What additional performance information is required that the COR cannot directly observe, measure, or obtain from the contractor?
- What information or data is the contractor expected to provide?
- What records and data must the supervisor provide?

4. *Make the vendor a partner in assessments.* Depending on the nature of the contract, the COR and supervisor may want to schedule regular meetings with the acquisition team, government supervisor, and contractor site managers. These meetings can be used as an opportunity to keep the entire team updated on the progress of the contract and serve as a venue for reviewing performance data. These meetings can also serve as opportunities for an informal exchange of ideas about the progress of the effort and may be helpful in identifying and preempting production problems. Regularly scheduled meetings can serve as a useful forum for discussing issues of concern and devising collaborative solutions to problems before they are formally identified as deficiencies.

5. *Validate the inspection methodology.* Once the inspection program is developed, it is important to beta test the methodology to ensure that it provides all data required to effectively assess the contractor's performance. There are a few key goals to keep in mind when assessing the inspection program.

- Are all performance criteria based on standards from the contract statement of work?
- Is the information easily gathered?
- Does it measure the right things?
- Does the inspection methodology provide a fair and accurate assessment of the contractor's performance?

6. *Adjust the inspection program as necessary.* Although it is generally better to maintain consistency in the data and metrics used to assess contractor performance, the COR and supervisor must be still be flexible in adjusting the inspection program if it is determined that different information is required or if the contractor's tasks change significantly. The supervisor and the COR should try to devise an evaluation system that is flexible, as government operations and requirements evolve. It is important to remember that any system designed to inspect, monitor, measure, and evaluate a contractor's performance must not unduly delay or inter-

fere with the contractor's accomplishment of their assigned tasks. Nor can the system of evaluation apply stricter standards of performance than those stated in the contract.

7. *Combine contractor inspections with periodic reviews of the government process.* It is important that the inspection program does not simply rely on a narrow view of the contractor's performance in isolation of external variables. There are certainly situations in which deficiencies in the government's process will have a detrimental impact on the contractor's ability to provide goods or services in accordance with the contract requirements. A holistic inspection program must take into account the effects of the government's own process on contractor operations. The supervisor and acquisition team must be aware of how inefficiencies in the government's internal processes or unique environmental conditions beyond the control of the contractor may impact the vendor's ability to satisfy the stated performance objectives. Inspection programs should consider some mechanism to take these issues into account and independently assess the government's own process efficiency as an integrated element of the contractor's total performance. Vendors must always bear responsibility for poor performance, but they should not be held accountable for deficiencies caused by operational flaws or failures in the government's design process.

8. *Establish procedures to document and report contractor performance.* As part of the surveillance plan, the contracting officer and the COR must also work with the supervisor to develop a clear and efficient mechanism for gathering information and documenting performance appraisals. While the COR has the primary function of conducting surveillance and evaluation duties, the supervisor plays an important part in facilitating inspections. In some cases the COR will not be continuously located at the site of performance and will rely on the supervisor to fill in information gaps between regularly scheduled performance reviews. Oftentimes the government supervisor or designated technical monitors will be tasked with collecting performance data relating to day-to-day operations.

It is important to remember that it is not the duty of the supervisor to evaluate or critique the contractor's performance. In all cases the supervisor should be communicating directly with the COR in relation to all observations concerning contractor performance. Below are a few issues that supervisors should discuss with the COR concerning how contractor-performance information will be documented and reported.

- Discuss who is responsible for evaluating and documenting contractor performance and what aspects of this responsibility will be delegated to technical monitors or other government employees.

- Determine what information should be included in the documentation of periodic performance reviews and assessments.
- Request examples of formatting for evaluations and discrepancy reports.
- Establish the frequency of reports and all required data.
- Ensure that each file for discrepancy reports includes information on the type of service being inspected; the identification of the inspector; the time, date, and circumstances of the observation; and a detailed statement as to what aspects of the contractor's performance did not satisfy the government's standards.
- Use statistical measures and specific examples from the contract to explain a discrepancy with the contractor's performance whenever possible.
- Discuss with the COR the expectations for record keeping and maintaining files relating to communications and evaluation of contractor performance.

9. *Have a plan for dealing with unsatisfactory contractor performance.* If the contract does not specifically address procedures for reporting unsatisfactory performance, be sure to discuss with the COR how this will occur. In most cases a deficiency report will be prepared by the COR and sent to the contracting officer to document a noted problem with the contractor's performance. A copy is typically provided to the vendor's site manager to make them aware of the issue.

At a minimum, discrepancy reports should include a description of the particular task or activity in which the problem was noted and some detail concerning how the contractor's performance deviated from the established standards of delivery. The COR may also include some comment relating to the government's intended actions or request that the vendor take specific actions to resolve the performance shortfall. Although these functions are primarily the responsibility of the COR, there should be procedures in place for the government supervisor to submit deficiency reports or complaints based on observed deficiencies. This may be through the formal mechanism of routine inspection reports or simply a memorandum of record noting the details of the deficiency observed by the supervisor.

It is important that the COR and the supervisor discuss documentation and reporting expectations in advance so that there is no confusion when the need arises. In most cases when a discrepancy is observed and reported the contractor should be provided an opportunity to respond to the complaint and provide a plan for remediation. Supervisors should be aware of the expectations and procedures for remediation and what actions will occur if improvements are not achieved.

10. *Account for the intangibles of a contractor's performance.* In addition to strictly statistical measures of contractor performance, there are numerous intangibles that should be considered as part of a holistic evaluation of the contractor's work. Some of these issues are difficult to quantify but still comprise an important element of successful partnerships and should be considered part of periodic assessments of a contractor's overall performance. Clearly there are many more issues than what is contained in the short list below, but these provide some general ideas about the kind of intangible inputs that contribute to a successful government-contractor partnership.

- honesty and integrity in dealing with workplace problems or performance issues
- promptness in dealing with personnel issues before they become disruptive to the workplace
- accurate and timely submission of reports, correspondence, and other required documentation
- quick and focused response to issues of concern noted by the supervisor, COR, or contracting officer
- positive attitude toward resolving performance deficiencies
- proactive solutions to potential problems before they are noted in formal surveillance reviews
- professionalism in workplace conduct and behavior
- proactive efforts to train employees not only to meet but also to exceed established government performance standards
- desire to engage in collaborative efforts with the government to seek process solutions, cost savings, and operational efficiencies
- effort to lower employee turnover and increase efficiency by providing a positive and rewarding work experience
- providing suggestions on integrating commercial sector best practices into the government's operation
- conducting careful recordkeeping, accounting, and documentation of quality control and performance data
- disciplined and honest conduct of internal reviews, quality-assurance programs, and audits
- attention to detail in managing employee personnel activities and performance
- proactive avoidance of problems relating to security and safety violations

Appendix A

Key Terms and Definitions in Acquisition and Contracting

THIS SHORT LIST of key definitions is by no means an exhaustive resource of acquisition and contracting terms. It is intended to provide the supervisor with basic terminology to help communicate with the acquisition team and vendor. For a more complete reference and legal definitions, consult the Federal Acquisition Regulations.

Acceptable quality level. The maximum percent defective that, for purposes of sampling inspections, may be considered satisfactory as a standard for delivery or goods or services. This measure is an element of the government's quality-assurance plan, used to assess whether the contractor's products or services meet requirements described in the performance work statement or statement of work.

Acquisition. A broad term encompassing the processes the government uses to obtain supplies or services through contracts or similar instruments such as purchase orders and ordering agreements. The contract agreement authorizes appropriated funds for supplies or services for government use through purchase or lease. Acquisition begins at the point when agency needs are established and includes the description of requirements, solicitation process, selection of sources, award of contract, financing, contract performance, administration procedures, and technical and managerial functions relating to the contract agreement.

Acquisition planning. The process by which the acquisition team coordinates a comprehensive plan for satisfying an identified government need through contract with a commercial provider. It includes the overall strategy for managing the acquisition and the steps involved with developing the contract and administering its execution.

Acquisition team. All participants in a government acquisition process including representatives of the technical and procurement communities as well as the customers they serve and the contractors who provide the products and services.

Administrative change. A unilateral contract modification that does not affect the substantive rights of the parties.

Amendment. A change in a solicitation prior to contract award.

Best value. The expected outcome of an acquisition that, in the government's estimation, provides the greatest overall benefit in response to the requirement. Best-value determinations are intended to ensure that the government makes good business decisions by including factors other than price, such as the probable life of the item selected, environmental and energy-efficiency considerations, and technical qualifications of schedule holders. Best-value determinations should consider the special features of the supply or service required for effective program performance, such as trade-in considerations, warranty considerations, and maintenance availability.

Bid. The process by which a contractor makes an offer to the government for goods or services during the acquisition process.

Blanket-purchase agreement (BPA). A contracting method used to speed up the acquisition process. A BPA is a nonbinding agreement between the government and a vendor that locks in prices without committing funding or obligating the government to purchase from a vendor. A BPA simplifies the acquisition process by reducing paperwork and expediting normal contracting requirements.

Change order. A written instruction signed by the contracting officer directing the contractor to make a change in the delivery of goods or services. The change clause in a contract may authorize the contracting officer to order changes without the contractor's consent.

Commercial activity. The process resulting in a product or service being obtained from a private-sector source.

Commercial item. Any item, other than real property, customarily used by the general public or by nongovernmental entities for nongovernmental purposes. This includes services offered and sold competitively in the commercial marketplace based on established market prices for specific tasks performed or specific outcomes to be achieved under standard commercial terms and conditions.

Commercial source. Any business or other concern that is eligible for contract award in accordance with Federal Acquisition Regulations.

Constructive change. A constructive change is any oral or written act by the contracting officer that is construed as having the same effect as a written change order.

Contract. A mutually binding legal relationship obligating a seller to furnish supplies or services and a buyer to pay for them. It includes all types of commitments that obligate the government to expenditure of appropriated funds. In addition to bilateral instruments, contracts include awards and notices of awards, job orders or task letters, letter contracts, and purchase orders.

Contract administration. Those activities performed by government officials after a contract has been awarded, encompassing all dealings between the government and the contractor from the time the contract is awarded until the work has been completed, accepted, or terminated, payments made, and disputes resolved. Contract administration is the part of the procurement process that assures that the government gets what it paid for. The focus is on obtaining supplies and services and on ensuring requisite quality and on-time delivery within budget estimates.

Contracting activity. An element of an agency, designated by the agency head, delegated broad authority regarding acquisition functions.

Contracting officer (CO or KO). A person duly appointed with the authority to enter into and administer contracts on behalf of the government. Serves as the government's authorized agent for all dealings and negotiations with contractors. The CO has sole authority to solicit proposals from vendors, negotiate terms of the agreement, and award and modify contracts on behalf of the government. In order to fulfill these functions, the CO requires assistance from technical advisors who help in the development of specific requirements, monitoring, and administrative responsibilities.

Contracting officer's representative (COR). Sometimes called the contracting officer's technical representative (COTR), the COR is an individual designated by the contracting officer to act as their representative for assisting in managing the contract. The authorities and limitations of a COR appointment are contained in the written letter of appointment. Among other duties, the COR verifies contractor performance, inspects contractor work, and maintains liaison and direct communication with the contractor. Contracting officers' representatives are required to complete mandatory training and continuing education in contract management and administration and are tasked to ensure that all contracted services are delivered to the government according to requirements specified in the contract language.

Contract specialist. Assists the contracting officer in pre-award, negotiation, contract-award, administration, and other required duties.

Cost-plus-award-fee contract. A cost-reimbursement-type contract that provides for a fee consisting of a base amount fixed at inception of the contract and an award amount that the contractor may earn based on performance factors, such as quality, timeliness, technical ingenuity, and cost-effective management. The amount of the award fee is determined by the government's judgmental evaluation of the contractor's performance in terms of criteria stated in the contract.

Cost-plus-fixed-fee contract. A cost-reimbursement-type contract providing for payment to the contractor of a negotiated fee fixed at the inception of the contract. The fixed fee does not vary with actual cost but may be adjusted as a result of changes in the work performed under the contract. This contract type permits contracting for efforts that might otherwise present too great a risk to contractors but provides the contractor only minimum incentive to control costs.

Cost-plus-incentive-fee contract. A cost-reimbursement-type contract providing for an initially negotiated fee to be adjusted later by a formula based on the relationship of total allowable costs to total target costs. This contract type specifies a target cost, a target fee, minimum and maximum fees, and a fee-adjustment formula. After contract performance, the fee payable to the contractor is determined in accordance with the formula. The formula provides, within limits, for increases in fees above the target fee when total allowable costs are less than target costs and decreases in fee when total allowable costs exceed target costs. This increase or decrease is intended to provide an incentive for the contractor to manage the contract effectively and seek efficiencies in operation.

Cost-reimbursement contract. A contract providing for payment of allowable incurred costs to the extent prescribed in the contract. These contracts establish an estimate of total cost for the purpose of obligating funds and establishing a ceiling that the contractor may not exceed (except at its own risk) without the approval of the contracting officer.

Customer feedback. A performance-assessment methodology applying first-hand information derived from actual users of the contractor-produced goods or services. It should be used to supplement other forms of evaluation and performance assessment. It may be especially useful for those types of services that do not lend themselves to traditional forms of assessment. This methodology tends to be subjective and nonstatistical in nature and therefore should not be relied on as the only method of performance assessment. Customer feedback is often complaint-oriented and may not always relate to actual requirements of the contract. Customer feedback should be validated through other forms of performance assessment.

Deficiency. A material failure to meet government requirements or a combination of significant weaknesses that increases the risk of unsuccessful contract performance to an unacceptable level.

Delivery order. An order for supplies placed against an established contract or with government sources.

Direct cost. Any cost that is identified specifically with a particular final cost objective. Direct costs are not limited to items that are incorporated in the end product, such as material or labor.

Excusable delay. A delay arising from causes beyond the control and without the fault or negligence of the contractor.

Fair and reasonable price. A contract allowing for appropriate cost risk in which a good contractor should be able to make a reasonable profit while satisfying the government's need.

Federal Acquisition Regulations (FAR). The principal set of rules in the Federal Acquisition Regulations System, consisting of regulations issued by agencies of the federal government describing the process through which the government purchases goods and services.

Firm fixed price, level of effort. The contractor is to provide a specified level of effort, over a stated period of time, on work that can be stated only in general terms, for which the government is to pay the contractor a fixed dollar amount.

Fixed price, award fee. A fixed price (including normal profit) for the contract effort. This price will be paid for satisfactory contract performance. An award fee will be paid (if earned) in addition to the fixed price. Periodic evaluation of the contractor's performance against an award-fee plan is required to determine the amount of fee (if any) due the contractor.

Fixed price contract. A contract that provides for a firm price or, in appropriate cases, an adjustable price. Fixed-price contracts providing for an adjustable price may include a ceiling price, a target price, or both. Unless otherwise specified in the contract, the ceiling price or target price is subject to adjustment only by operation of contract clauses providing for an equitable adjustment or other revision of the contract price under stated circumstances.

Fixed price, economic adjustment. A contract that provides for upward and downward revision of the stated contract price with economic price dependent on the occurrence of specified contingencies. Economic price may be adjusted based on established prices, actual costs of labor or material, or cost indexes of labor or material.

Full and open competition. The concept that any reasonable offer made to the government for goods or services should be allowed to compete. In certain cases the government may impose certain socioeconomic parameters, limiting full and open competition.

Government-furnished property. Government property delivered or otherwise made available to the contractor for use in execution of the contract. Government property may be incorporated into or attached to a deliverable end item or may be consumed or expended in performing a contract. Property includes assemblies, components, parts, raw and processed materials, and small tools and supplies.

GSA advantage. An online shopping service that enables ordering offices to search product information, review delivery options, place orders directly with contractors, and pay contractors for orders using the government commercial-purchase card.

Indefinite-delivery contract. A contract that may be used to acquire supplies or services when the exact times or quantities of future deliveries are not known at the time of contract award. There are three types of indefinite delivery contracts: definite-quantity contracts, requirement contracts, and indefinite-quantity contracts. Also known as task orders (for services) and delivery orders (for supplies).

Indefinite-quantity contract. An indefinite-delivery contract that provides for an indefinite quantity, within stated limits, of supplies or services to be furnished during a fixed period, with deliveries or performance scheduled by placing orders with the contractor.

Information security. Refers to protecting of information and information systems from unauthorized access, use, disclosure, disruption, modification, or destruction of information. Information security provides for information integrity, which means guarding against improper information modification or destruction, and includes ensuring information nonrepudiation and authenticity; confidentiality, which means preserving authorized restrictions on access and disclosure, including means for protecting personal privacy and proprietary information; and availability, which means ensuring timely and reliable access to, and use of, information.

Inherently governmental functions. Functions intimately related to the public interest as to mandate performance by government employees. These functions include those activities requiring either the exercise of discretion in applying government authority or value judgments in making decisions for the government. Governmental functions normally fall into two categories: the act of governing (the discretionary exercise of government authority) and monetary transactions and entitlements. Some examples of inherently governmental functions include direct conduct of criminal investigations, prosecutions and adjudication, command of military forces, conduct of foreign relations and determination of foreign policy, determination of agency policy and content of regulations, determination of program priorities and budgets, direction and control of federal employees, drafting congressional testimony, responses to congressional correspondence, and agency responses to audit reports.

Market research. The step during the acquisition process where the acquisition team gathers and analyzes information about capabilities of the market (goods or services) to satisfy a particular government need.

Modification. A written change to the terms of the contract. A modification may be unilateral (initiated by the government) or bilateral (in agreement of both contract parties).

Nonpersonal-services contract. A contract under which the personnel rendering the services are not subject, either by the contract's terms or by the manner of its administration, to the supervision and control typically prevailing in relationships between the government and its employees.

Option. A unilateral right by the government for which, during a specified time, the government may elect to purchase additional supplies or services called for in the contract or may elect to extend the contract.

Organizational conflict of interest. A situation that exists when the nature of work to be performed under a proposed government contract may, without some restriction on future activities, result in an unfair competitive advantage to the contractor or impair the contractor's objectivity in performing the work.

Outsourcing. The transfer of a support function traditionally performed by an in-house organization to an outside service provider. Outsourcing occurs in both the public and private sectors. While the outsourcing firm or government organization continues to provide appropriate oversight, the vendor is typically granted a degree of flexibility regarding how the work is performed. In successful outsourcing arrangements, the vendor utilizes new technologies and business practices to improve service delivery and/or to reduce support costs. Vendors are usually selected as the result of an open competition among qualified bidders.

Past performance. The government policy of keeping track of how well a contractor performs a contract or service. It is used to assess the risk of using the same contractor on similar projects in the future.

Performance-assessment personnel or quality-assurance personnel. May also be referred to as quality-assurance evaluators (QAE), contracting officers' representatives (COR), or contracting officers' technical representatives (COTR), but the duties are essentially the same. They serve as the on-site technical managers assessing contractor performance against defined performance standards. Performance-assessment personnel are responsible for researching the marketplace to remain current with the most efficient and effective performance-assessment methods and techniques.

Performance-assessment plan. Describes the plan for how government personnel will evaluate and assess contractor performance. The document should be revised or modified as circumstances warrant. It is based on the premise that the contractor, not the government, is primarily responsible for managing and ensuring that quality controls meet the terms of the contract. A performance-assessment plan should be incorporated into the contract agreement and furnished to the contractor.

Performance-based service acquisition (PBSA). Encompasses a variety of acquisition strategies, methods, and techniques that focus on measurable outcomes rather than directive performance processes. They are structured around defining the service requirement in terms of general performance objectives, then providing contractors with latitude to determine how best to satisfy the government's requirements.

Performance measures. A series of indicators, expressed in qualitative, quantitative, or other tangible terms, that determines if a vendor's performance is reasonable and cost-effective. Performance measures can include workload estimates, output-to-cost ratios, transaction ratios, error rates, consumption rates, inventory fill rates, timeliness measures, completion and back order rates, and the like. Quality service measures may include responsiveness rates, user-satisfaction rates, and so on.

Performance requirement. The defined measure that divides acceptable and unacceptable performance.

Performance standard. Reflects the minimum, sector-specific requirement for the performance of a commercial activity, incorporating both quality measures and cost measures. Cost measures reflect cost comparability to assure equity in the comparison of performance standards with private-industry standards.

Performance-work statement (PWS). A statement of the technical, functional, and performance characteristics of the work performed by a contractor. It identifies essential functions to be performed and determines performance factors, including the location of the work, the units of work, the quantity of work units, quality, and timeliness. It serves as the scope of work and is the basis for all assessed costs in a contract.

Periodic sampling. A performance-assessment methodology similar to random sampling but planned at specific intervals or dates. It may be appropriate for tasks that occur infrequently. Selecting this tool to determine a contractor's compliance with contract requirements can be effective since it permits assessment of the contractor's performance without consuming a significant amount of time or resources for surveillance.

Personal-services contract. A contract that, by its express terms or as administered, makes contractor personnel appear, in effect, to be government employees. Except for certain specific circumstances outlined in the Federal Acquisition Regulation, the government generally only contracts for nonpersonal services. In simple terms, this means that the government cannot hire contractors to be used interchangeably with government employees, nor can supervisors exercise similar management controls over contractor personnel as they would government employees. Some factors indicating the possible existence of a personal-services contract include performance of work on site at a government office; use of tools and equipment furnished by the government; services applied directly to the integral effort of an agency or organization; comparable services performed in other agencies using civil service personnel; services provided that can reasonably be expected to last beyond one year; services that inherently require government direction or supervision of contractor employees in order to protect government interest or retain control of the function involved; work that places a contractor in a position of command, supervision, administration, or control over government personnel or the personnel of other contractors; or performance of contractor duties that gives the appearance that the contractor is part of the government organization.

Privatization. The process of changing a public entity or enterprise to private control and ownership. It does not include either determinations as to whether a support service should be obtained through public or private resources or those cases when the government retains full responsibility and control over the delivery of those services.

Procurement Integrity Act. This act prohibits the release of source selection, contractor bid, or proposal information. It also prohibits former government employees, who served in certain positions on procurement actions or contracts in excess of $10 million, from receiving compensation as an employee or consultant of that contractor for a period of one year.

Proprietary data. Information that belongs to a contractor and applies to manufacturing processes, operations, or techniques that may distinguish that firm from its competition. This information must be labeled and protected by the government from unauthorized release.

Protest. A written objection made by an interested party to the solicitation for a proposed contract for acquisition of services or supply. The objection is to some term of the proposed award or contract.

Purchase order. Order issued by the government to buy supplies or services on specified terms and conditions, using simplified acquisition procedures.

Quality-assurance evaluator. An employee responsible for surveillance of contractor or government performance.

Quality-assurance surveillance. The methodology in performance-based service acquisitions by which government employees supervise in-house or contract performance to ensure that the standards of the performance work statement are satisfied.

Quality-assurance-surveillance plan (QASP). A document used for quality assurance containing specific plans and methods for performing surveillance of the contractor, including written instructions by which the COR ensures that the government is getting what is contractually required. The QASP should contain a checklist of performance items extracted from the statement of work or statement of objectives. The QASP is based on the premise that the contractor, and not the government, is responsible for management and quality control actions to meet the terms of the contract.

Quality control. Those actions taken by a contractor to control the performance of services so that they meet the requirements of the performance work statement or statement of work.

Random sampling. A statistically based assessment method for quality assurance that assumes acceptable contractor performance based on a certain percentage or number of scheduled assessments found to be acceptable. The results of these assessments help the government determine if performance is marginal or unsatisfactory. Satisfactory or exceptional performance can be the basis for adjusting the sample size or sampling frequency. Random sampling is an appropriate surveillance methodology for frequently recurring tasks. It works best when the number of instances is very large and a statistically valid sample can be reasonably obtained.

Solicitation. Any request to submit offers to the government for the provision of goods or services by a commercial vendor. Solicitations under negotiated procedures are called *requests for proposals (RFP).* Solicitations under simplified acquisition procedures may require submission of either a quotation or an offer.

Source-selection information. Information used by an agency for the purpose of evaluating a bid or proposal for a government-procurement contract. This information is considered sensitive and should not be shared with vendors or potential bidders for government contracts. This includes information such as bid prices submitted in response to an agency invitation for bids; proposed costs or prices submitted in response to an agency solicitation; source-selection plans; technical-evaluation plans; technical evaluations of proposals;

cost or price evaluations of proposals; competitive determinations on proposals being considered for award of a contract; rankings of bids, proposals, or competitors; reports and evaluations of source-selection panels, boards, or advisory councils; or other information marked as source-selection information. See the Federal Acquisition Regulations for additional information on appropriate handling of this information.

Statement of objectives. A document incorporated into the solicitation that states the overall performance objectives of the contract. It is used in solicitations when the government intends to provide maximum flexibility for the contractor to use innovative approaches. It is the preferred manner of describing the government's requirements under performance-based service-acquisitions methodology.

Statement of work (SOW). Defines requirements in clear, concise language identifying specific work to be accomplished. It also defines the respective responsibilities of the government and the contractor and provides objective measures so that both the government and the contractor will know when the work is complete and payment justified.

Stop-work order. A contract clause permitting the government to order the contractor to stop work if required for reasons such as advancement in state-of-the-art production or engineering breakthroughs, or realignment of programs. Generally, a stop-work order will be issued only if it is advisable to suspend work pending a decision by the government and a supplemental agreement providing for the suspension is not feasible. Issuance of a stop-work order must be approved at a level higher than the contracting officer.

Surveillance plan. A guide describing the contract-monitoring methods, written by the acquisition team as the work statement is developed. It is used by the COR in managing oversight of contract performance. It is generally mandatory for time and material contracts. Simple delivery contracts do not require a surveillance plan.

Suspension. An action taken by an authorized official temporarily disqualifying a contractor from government contracting and government-approved subcontracting.

Task-order contract. An order for services placed against an established contract or with a government source. Does not procure or specify a firm quantity of services (other than a minimum or maximum quantity) and provides for the issuance of orders for the performance of tasks during the period of the contract.

Task orders. Any number of instruments used to order services under a task-order contract. Task orders are always prepared by a contracting officer and are part of the contract file and the COR file.

Termination. The cancellation of all or part of the work that has not been completed and accepted under contract. It may, under specific circumstances, be for default of the contractor or for convenience of the government.

Termination for convenience. The exercise of the government's right to completely or partially terminate performance of work under a contract when it is in the government's interest.

Termination for default. The exercise of the government's right to completely or partially terminate a contract because of the contractor's actual or anticipated failure to perform its contractual obligations.

Third-party audits. A method of performance assessment where contractor evaluation is conducted by an outside third-party organization that is independent of the government and the contractor. All documentation supplied to, and produced by, the third party should be made available to both the government and the contractor.

Time-and-materials contract. A contracting method providing for acquisition of supplies or services on the basis of direct labor hours at specified fixed hourly rates that include wages, overhead, general and administrative expenses, and profit for the vendor. A ceiling price is established, which the contractor may not exceed. Substantial surveillance on the government's part is required to insure that inefficient methods are not used.

Trend analysis. A performance-assessment method used on a continual basis to track a contractor's performance over time. Various sampling methods such as random and periodic inspections can be used to gather performance information. Databases and statistical tools can be developed to analyze trends in performance or output. Contractor-managed metrics may also provide additional information used in the analysis.

Unallowable cost. Any cost that, under the provisions of pertinent law, regulation, or contract, cannot be included in prices, cost reimbursements, or settlements under a government contract.

Unauthorized commitment. An agreement that is nonbinding because the representative making it lacked the authority to enter into the agreement on behalf of the government. This usually occurs when a contractor relies on the apparent authority of a government official who does not have the authority to obligate the government contractually. If the actual approval authority does not ratify the unauthorized commitment, the person who caused it may be held personally and financially liable. Even if the action is eventually ratified, the person who caused it may be subjected to administrative or other penalties.

Appendix B

Checklist for Analysis and Review of Service Contracts

THE FOLLOWING CHECKLIST is derived from the Office of Federal Procurement Policy (OFPP) Policy letter 93-1, concerning Management Oversight of Service Contracting. The policy letter offers a useful methodology for conducting analysis and review of a proposed service contract. Use the following questions to ensure that a proposed service contract is appropriately developed and administered.

Appropriateness of Commercial Performance

Is the required service an inherently governmental function? If the response is affirmative, the contract requirement is for a function that must be performed by government officials.

Weighing Cost-Effectiveness Factors

Consider the following questions to determine if the requiring activity has a valid need and is satisfying the requirement in the most cost-effective manner.

☐ Is the statement of work properly written so as to clearly support the need for the specified service?

☐ Is the statement of work properly written so as to permit adequate cost-comparison evaluation of contractor versus in-house performance?

☐ Is the choice of contract type, quality assurance plan, competition strategy, or other related acquisition strategy and procedure appropriate to ensure a good contract management and oversight?

☐ If a cost-reimbursement contract is contemplated, is the acquisition plan adequate to address the proper type of cost reimbursement, ensuring that the contractor will have the incentive to control costs under the contract?

☐ Is the cost estimate, or other supporting cost information, adequate to enable the contracting office to effectively determine whether costs are reasonable?

☐ Is the statement of work adequate to describe the requirement in terms of what is to be performed as opposed to how the work will be accomplished?

☐ Is the acquisition plan adequate to ensure that there is proper consideration given to quality and best-value determinations?

Maintaining Appropriate Government Controls

Consider the following questions to determine if a proposed contract is sufficient to maintain appropriate government controls.

☐ Are there sufficient government resources to evaluate contractor performance if the statement of work requires the contractor to provide advice, analysis and evaluation, opinions, alternatives, or recommendations that could significantly influence agency policy development or decision making?

☐ Is the quality-assurance plan sufficient to adequately monitor contractor performance?

☐ Is the statement of work properly written so that it clearly specifies a contract deliverable or requires some method of progress reporting on contractor performance?

☐ Is there concern that the agency lacks the expertise to independently evaluate the contractor's approach, methodology, results, options, conclusions, or recommendations?

Determining Potential Conflicts of Interests

Use the following questions to identify potential conflict-of-interest problems.

- ☐ Can the potential bidder devise solutions or make recommendations that would influence the award of future contracts to that contractor?
- ☐ If the requirement is for support services, were any potential bidders involved in developing the system design specifications?
- ☐ Have the potential bidders participated in earlier work involving the same program or activity that is the subject of the present contract wherein the bidders have access to source selection or proprietary information not available to other bidders competing for the contract?
- ☐ Will the contractor be evaluating a competitor's work?
- ☐ Does the contract allow the contractor to accept its own products or activities on behalf of the government?
- ☐ Will the work under contract put the contractor in a position to influence government decision making, such as developing regulations that will affect the contractor's current or future business?
- ☐ Will the work under contract affect the interests of the contractor's other clients?
- ☐ Are any potential bidders, or personnel who will perform the contract, former agency officials who personally and substantially participated in the development of the requirement or the procurement of these services within the past two years?

Determine Appropriate Contract Competition

Use the following questions to determine if appropriate consideration was given to open-market competition.

- ☐ Is the statement of work narrowly defined, or does it have excessively restrictive specifications and performance standards?
- ☐ Is the contract formulated in such a way as to create a continuous and dependent arrangement with the same contractor?
- ☐ Is the use of an indefinite quantity or term-contract arrangement inappropriate to obtain the required services?
- ☐ Will the requirement be obtained through the use of other than full and open competition?

Appendix C

Tips for Preparing a
Performance Work Statement (PWS)

T HE FOLLOWING TIPS for preparing a PBSA performance work statement were derived in part from the Department *of Defense Guidebook for Performance-Based Services Acquisition* (March 2001).

Particularly with PBSA methodology, the acquisition team should make significant use of the expertise and experience of government supervisors and other subject matter experts during preparation of the performance work statements. These tips provide the supervisor with a general understanding to help them prepare their contributions to the work of the acquisition team.

Key Objectives for Writing the Performance Work Statement (PWS)

- Express the government's desired outcome in clear, simple, concise, results-oriented, measurable, and legally enforceable terms.
- Use a format that presents the specified tasks in an easily understood manner.
- Determine what exhibits will help convey to the contractor the job that needs to be done.

Key Elements of a PWS

A PWS should contain several key elements to help the contractor understand the nature of the requirement.

- *Introduction.* An overall statement of the required services in terms of outcome. It should describe major program goals and desired results.
- *Scope of work and conditions of performance.* Additional information that further clarifies the specific performance objectives. This section should briefly describe the purpose of the current work and the desired outcome. It should also establish such general requirements as place of performance, work hours, details of required services, special vendor qualifications, etc.
- *Measurable performance standards or workload indicators.* Performance standards may be expressed as an acceptable quality level (AQL) for each outcome. Workload indicators may also be used to describe the output in terms of volume effort or production levels.
- *Time frame or milestones.* Time lines or major milestones for when the requirement must be completed in part or whole.
- *Quality-assurance-surveillance plan (QASP).* The government's inspection plan providing a detailed description of the methods that will be used to measure performance in accordance with the requirements and performance standards in the PWS.

Establishing Performance Measures in the PWS

There are several ways to measure contractor performance in the development of the PWS. Some key things that must be considered in determining how performance will be measured follow.

- *Economy.* Obtaining the desired quality or quality at the best price.
- *Efficiency.* The contractor's best use of available resources.
- *Effectiveness.* How well was the government's objective accomplished?

Some Examples of Performance Standards for a PWS

- Response times, delivery times, timeliness, meeting deadlines or due dates, adherence to schedule.

- Error rates or accuracy rates. Number of mistakes or errors permitted by the performance standard.
- Completion milestone rates. The percentage of a project or effort complete at a given date.
- Cost controls. Keeping within the estimated cost or target cost. Applies in cost reimbursement contract arrangement.

Preparing a PWS for Support Services Contracts

A performance work statement (PWS) for support services will generally describe all the pertinent work to be performed, along with measurements for adequate work performance, evaluation and assessment techniques, and incentives as applicable. Below are the common elements of a performance work statement.

- introduction detailing the statement of objectives
- scope of work
- requirements and performance standards
- contract deliverables
- data requirements
- applicable appendixes

Preparing a PWS for a Research and Development Contract

Many research and development efforts and other service contracts that are conceptual in nature focus on abstract objectives where outcomes are difficult to describe precisely in advance. Performance work statements for these types of projects and services can be challenging to develop. Consider breaking the effort into suboutcomes or phases. The PWS should provide flexibility to allow for innovation and creativity.

In basic research, emphasis will normally focus on limited rather than ultimate objectives. In basic research programs where results cannot be determined in advance, no deliverable is required except a final report. In these cases objective performance standards cannot be set. The proper procurement vehicle is usually a cooperative agreement rather than a contract. Following is a sample outline:

- introduction
- scope of work

- description of tasks to be performed and performance standards
- schedule
- reporting requirements
- attachments, appendixes, and exhibits as required

Language-Usage Tips for Writing Good Performance Work Statements

The PWS will be read and interpreted by a variety of personnel from diverse disciplines. The words must be understood not only by the drafters but also by all readers, including government employees from nonacquisition backgrounds. Potential vendors offering proposals to the government must interpret words within the PWS to estimate costs, develop plans, and determine anticipated profit. Therefore, each requirement must be communicated to the reader in a clear, concise, correct, and complete manner.

- *Style.* The method used in expressing ideas in phrases, sentences, and paragraphs. Strive to include all essential information in a concise, accurate, thorough, and logical sequence, with clear, simple presentation. Avoid the use of complex words, acronyms, and government jargon.
- *Sentences.* Eliminate long, complicated sentences by rearranging them into shorter, simpler phrases expressing a single thought or idea. Avoid sentences with legal phrases, technical jargon, government acronyms, and other elaborate phrases. Eliminate unnecessary words from sentences, and omit unnecessary sentences from paragraphs.
- *Paragraphs.* A paragraph may consist of one or more sentences, discussing a single idea or like ideas. State the main idea in the first or topic sentence at the beginning of the paragraph to allow readers to grasp the meaning immediately. The topic sentence provides a base for subsequent sentences in developing and supporting the main idea. Avoid long paragraphs if possible, since they may crowd ideas and confuse the reader.
- *Language usage.* Use the active voice rather than the passive. Active writing uses action verbs that illustrate the subject as performing rather than receiving the action verb. The active voice is nearly always clearer and more direct than the passive, resulting in fewer words without reducing clarity of technical and contractual intent. Use of the active voice makes the subject (the contractor) responsible and accountable for the action or performance required.
- *Punctuation.* Use minimal punctuation to keep the PWS clear. Since the goal is to write simple, short, concise sentences, a well-written document

should require minimum punctuation. When complicated punctuation is required, consider rewriting the sentence instead. Construct sentences so that inadvertent misplacement or elimination of a punctuation mark will not alter the intended meaning. For maximum possible clarity, follow formal rules of punctuation.

- *Abbreviations and acronyms.* Due to the significant use of these in government-agency documents and writing, many misunderstandings may arise from commercial vendors' unfamiliarity with the terms. Remember always to define the abbreviations and acronyms at first use. When there are many abbreviations or acronyms in a contract, be sure to prepare a glossary in an annex.
- *Redundancy and repetition.* Avoid redundancy and unnecessary repetition. They reduce clarity and increase the likelihood of ambiguity, inconsistency, and internal contradiction.

Questions to Ask about the Performance Work Statement

After a draft performance work statement is prepared, there are several questions that must be asked to evaluate the quality of the PWS. It is important to remember that the PWS is being written for the contractor as much as for the government. These questions should be considered from the contractor's point of view. If the PWS does not convey a clear description of the government's requirements and expected standards, there is little chance that a contractor will be able to develop realistic cost estimates and proposals for a bid on the project. Apply the questions below to validate the quality of the performance work statement.

- Will the contractor be able to prepare a sound technical proposal based on the information provided in the PWS?
- Are the government's desired outcomes clearly stated so that the contractor understands exactly what to do, what must be delivered, and when it is required?
- Are the tasks realistic and performable?
- Will a contractor be able to prepare an accurate cost estimate from the information provided?
- Is the PWS sufficiently detailed to enable both the government and the contractor to estimate labor and other material costs, as well as to identify additional resources required for accomplishing the task?
- Are standards clearly identified in such a way that all parties can adequately measure performance?

- Is the PWS too restrictive or too focused on telling the contractor how to do their work?
- Are proper quantities and delivery dates indicated for each deliverable?
- Are schedules and frequencies of performance clearly defined?
- Are all required references and other documents provided?
- Have the appropriate government and industry standards been researched and referenced in the PWS?
- Have all necessary data requirements and/or technical specifications been provided?
- Are inspection methods, procedures, and standards described?

Appendix D

Tips for Writing a Statement of Work

T HE FOLLOWING INFORMATION provides some basic tips for preparing a contract statement of work (SOW). While the government supervisor will not be responsible for preparing contract language, often they will provide significant assistance to the contracting officer and acquisition team in preparation of the requirements language, including the statement of work describing the expectations for contractor performance. It is important that the supervisor understand the qualities of a well-written statement of work. This will enable them to be a more informed reader of the existing contract and improve communication with the COR and vendor in order to maximize the efficiency and performance of the blended team.

A contract statement of work describes a service requirement in terms of outputs, required quality levels, or standards of performance. The SOW tells the prospective contractor what needs to be accomplished. A well-written SOW should provide the contractor with everything needed to develop a proposal and to estimate costs associated with providing a particular service to the government. A SOW should also facilitate effective contract administration, oversight, and surveillance.

The SOW is the guideline for both the contractor and the supervisor describing the nature of the contractor's performance. It should be the primary reference document for the government supervisor to understand what the contractor should be contributing to accomplishment of the agency or organizational mission. The SOW will be the reference document used by the COR to resolve disputes between the government and the contractor.

Basic Elements of the Statement of Work

There is no set formula for the statement of work, but there are some basic elements that are common to most requirements. At a minimum, the following items should be addressed in the SOW.

- *Scope of work.* Describes the nature of the work to be performed, including any work plan, required deliverables, and performance standards.
- *Period of performance.* Provides a start and end date for the entire project and any other intermediate goals for key milestones and delivery timelines.
- *Physical location.* A description of the place where work will be performed. This may also include any relevant information on the environment of performance. This is particularly important for contingency contracting or work in deployed locations.
- *Supplies and equipment.* List all supplies and equipment that will be used in the execution of the contract. It is important to clarify government-furnished equipment versus those materials that must be provided by the contractor.
- *Payment rate.* This describes cost estimates and the dollar amount for all goods and services.
- *Delivery standards or acceptance criteria.* A description of the expected quality level and standards determining whether or not the product or service is acceptable.
- *Total not to exceed.* Total dollar amount of the award.
- *Special requirements.* Other aspects of the requirement including required hardware or software, specialized workforce qualifications, mandatory training or certifications for contractor personnel, travel requirements, special safety and/or security requirements, and anything else not covered in the body of the contract.

Tips for Writing a Good Statement of Work

Below are some general writing tips to help in the preparation of a clear, concise, and descriptive statement of work. Quality writing is critical for avoiding uncertainty in interpretation of the government's requirement and will help avoid disputes between the government and the contractor.

The bottom line for preparing the statement of work is that it must be clear enough to let the contractor know what he or she must do, definitive enough to protect the government's interests, and complete enough to provide meaningful measures of performance so that work is done to standard. One mnemonic device for evaluating the effectiveness of a statement of work is the SMART test. Ensuring that the SOW is

Specific in descriptions of requirements
Measurable in standards of delivery
Accountable for surveillance, oversight, and performance
Reasonable in expectations for government requirements and contractor profits
Time-based in setting standards for delivery

Some Other Tips for Writing Statements of Work

- Try to use plain and simple language, avoiding jargon, vague terms, and rambling sentences. Simple words, phrases, and sentences are used for clarity.
- Do not excessively use technical language, government acronyms, and abbreviations. Remember to spell out acronyms and provide definitions for any technical or unique terms.
- Do not expect to cover all possible contingencies. Keep the descriptions brief, clear, and to the point.
- Try to avoid overlap, repetition, and duplication. Redundancy can reduce clarity, resulting in ambiguity and contradiction.
- Use generic (nonproprietary) terminology in describing the requirements. This will avoid giving the appearance that the contract language is biased toward a particular contractor or proprietary processes.
- Be aware that the words *will* and *shall* have specific legal meanings within a SOW. The word *shall* is used to convey a binding provision. Use *shall* when describing a provision binding on the contractor. Use *will* to indicate actions to be conducted by the government.
- Avoid overly specific descriptions of processes that will restrict how the contractor will do their work. This may limit variation and flexibility in the contract and require later modifications if the government's needs change.
- Pay attention to verb choice. Use active verbs. Avoid passive verbs that can lead to vague statements.
- Avoid using the words *should* or *may* because they leave the decision for action up to the contractor.
- Terminology must be consistent throughout the document to reduce the possibility of misinterpretation.

- Ensure that services requested in the contract are not inherently governmental functions.
- Use commercial-sector terms when possible rather than government-only terminology.
- Avoid using the words *any, either,* or *and/or,* unless the intent is to give the contractor a choice in what must be done.
- Ensure that any document referenced in the SOW is furnished in the contract or the location of the original source clearly identified and available for reference.

Appendix E

Considerations for Contingency Contracting

A GREAT DEAL OF THE RECENT EXPANSION in government-service contracting has occurred within the context of contingency operations, such as overseas support to military operations or domestic emergencies like Hurricane Katrina recovery and other disaster-relief support. Generally speaking, contingency contracting occurs as a result of unplanned emergencies, such as disaster relief operations, response to terrorism, civil disturbance incidents, or military operations.

The unpredictable nature of these events places significant demands on government planners and acquisition specialists, requiring them to proactively develop detailed support requirements. Oftentimes this planning must be conducted with limited information as to the scale, scope, and type of commercial augmentation required. Government planners must develop best estimates based on analysis of historical case studies and scenario-driven war-gaming exercises in order to develop requirements against hypothetical contingencies. This proactive approach to acquisition planning is necessary in order to provide an efficient and orderly process when unexpected contingency scenarios do arise and commercial augmentation is required.

The tips below offer a general guide for conducting a mission analysis of future contingency operations and developing contract-support requirements. While many variables will remain unknown, the process of mission analysis will help planners determine the general nature of their contracting requirements prior to the event of crisis. This proactive approach will enable acquisition team members and government supervisors to better react to contingency scenarios and to develop draft requirements language and cost estimates prior to the event of crisis. Proactive planning will save the government time, money, and administrative burdens during the contingency-response phase.

1. Examine the range of possible agency missions and functions as part of a hypothetical contingency or crisis event. Use this information, as well as historical case studies of previous contingency operations, to develop most-likely scenarios.
2. Conduct a mission analysis to determine essential services likely to be required for each of the proposed contingency scenarios. This analysis should include a detailed review of expected support needs, man-hour requirements, special skill sets, and other services that are likely to be required during the contingency.
3. Develop a listing of specified and implied tasks that must be accomplished for each scenario.
4. Determine planning assumptions and variables for each scenario.
5. Establish reasonable limits and constraints on time and resources that are available for each scenario.
6. Determine the likely duration of support requirements for each scenario, and use these estimates to develop budgeting figures and projected costs.
7. Determine what policies, regulations, or legal restrictions may apply to each scenario. For this part of the analysis it is helpful to include a contracting and/or legal specialist on the planning team.
8. Determine potential risks and opportunities associated with using commercial-augmentation support for each scenario. Determine if any critical functions cannot be performed by contractor support due to legal restrictions or acquisition regulations.
9. Be sure to take into consideration any secondary-support requirements for the contract workforce. Include such items as transportation, housing, food, medical care, and security. Under normal contracting procedures, such support requirements would typically be the responsibility of the vendor to provide for their employees, but in various contingency scenarios a vendor cannot always be reasonably expected to provide for all life-support functions. Government planners must take these variables into account, particularly when planning for the initial phases of a crisis response.
10. Once various courses of action are developed, planners should war-game each scenario in order to determine how selected variables and assumptions will impact the support requirements and the ability to effectively employ contractor support.

11. Based on the results of the war-gaming exercise, develop a revised list of requirements for each scenario. Use these preliminary requirements to create draft-contract clauses, cost-estimate assumptions, and other planning estimates prior to initiation of actual operations.
12. Determine preferred contract types and vehicles most appropriate for the services required.
13. Develop generic requirements language and statements of work for services likely to be required.
14. Develop an idea of the necessary administrative controls that will be required to manage the contractor workforce in each contingency scenario. This should include estimates for the number of government-oversight personnel to perform administrative and surveillance functions. Develop estimates for total numbers of contract-support personnel, contract administrators, COR, and COTR based on various scenarios. Identify various sourcing options to obtain contract-administration personnel on short notice from other agencies and organizations.
15. Based on a revised analysis of contingency scenarios, develop a detailed list of skill sets, services, specialized training and prerequisites that are likely to be required from potential vendors.
16. Develop standards for delivery and performance measures based on study of prior contingency operations.
17. Conduct preliminary market research to develop a list of potential vendors for various contingency scenarios. If appropriate, set up draft contracts in advance for contingency-support functions.
18. Submit all draft estimates, contract language, and requirements for legal and budget review prior to initiation of contingency operations.

Appendix F

Contract Support in Forward Locations or Austere Environments

---

SUPERVISING A MIXED government-contractor workforce in forward locations or austere environments presents an entirely different set of challenges for the supervisor. Issues such as contractor integration, life support, medical care, housing, and security are added management considerations that require proactive planning on the part of the entire acquisition team. Consideration for these issues must occur in advance and be explicitly outlined in the contract language.

Below are some items to consider for government planners developing contract vehicles for commercial augmentation in nonstandard or austere environments.

1. If operating outside the United States, planners must consider certain host nation limitations on contractor support that may not apply to government-sponsored personnel. Issues may include differing entry and visa requirements, local income taxation, driving permits, insurance coverage, host nation legal restrictions, and potential liability concerns in criminal proceedings. If contractors are supporting military operations it is important to review the host nation Status of Forces Agreements (SOFA) to be aware of any specific stipulations with regard to contractors accompanying the force. Be aware of issues regarding visa limitations, criminal jurisdictions, travel restrictions, work permits, or other concerns specifically related to contractor

personnel operating in a foreign country supporting U.S. government organizations.

2. If supporting a military operation, supervisors must be aware of all contractor legal liabilities under the Uniform Code of Military Justice (UCMJ), the Military Extraterritorial Jurisdiction Act (MEJA), or host nation Status of Forces Agreements (SOFA).

3. Plan for overseas transportation requirements and onward movement inside the foreign country for transportation of contractor support to the site of performance. This is particularly a concern in a nonpermissive security situation or in emergency-relief operations where environmental conditions may not reasonably permit the vendor to transport their own employees to the site of performance.

4. Consider potential safety and environmental concerns possibly inhibiting the ability of the contractor to perform their work. Certain conditions may require additional training or specialized preparation, such as antiterrorism awareness training or unique security precautions, in order to safeguard the contractor workforce. Generally speaking, the government does not assume responsibility for protecting contractors, particularly in domestic locations or permanent overseas facilities such as military posts, embassies, or other government compounds, but certain exceptions exist for contingency environments. In these circumstances the government will generally be expected to provide force-protection measures equivalent to those afforded to government employees. At the very least, the government will likely furnish the minimum force-protection services necessary for contractors to perform their duties as defined by the contract. In such scenarios, contractor employees are expected to adhere to policies and regulations similar to that of government employees in order to facilitate necessary security operations. To ensure compliance, it is important for the contract language to be specifically tailored to include expected restrictions that are appropriate to the operational environment. Ultimately, contractors are only required to abide by the terms of the contract, federal criminal law, and applicable rules of the host nation. If additional guidelines are not explicitly stipulated in the contract, supervisors may have difficulty enforcing compliance on the part of the contractor unless their conduct inhibits them from performing duties required under contract.

5. Consider any special arrangements for food, lodging, equipment, clothing, and local medical support as required.

6. Plan for special management controls appropriate for local security or environmental hazards.

7. Consider special requirements for medical or mortuary evacuation.

8. Coordinate for identification and credentialing requirements such as foreign driver's licenses, visas, identification cards, Geneva Convention cards, etc.

9. Ensure that contractor personnel are carefully screened and medically cleared if they will be working in an austere environment with limited life support or medical services.

10. Provide clear guidance regarding contractor conduct for issues such as weapons usage, leisure travel, consumption of alcohol, social or business interactions with local nationals, or other security considerations that may adversely impact government operations.

11. Determine if there are requirements for counterintelligence or counterespionage considerations for those contractors performing operationally sensitive functions or work on classified programs. This is particularly a concern in overseas environments where there is increased counterintelligence risk.

12. Include contractor personnel as part of noncombatant evacuation planning and procedures.

13. Determine the criteria for mission-essential contractor personnel in the event of crisis situation or mandatory noncombatant evacuation.

14. Develop a plan for the continuation of vital services in the event of evacuation of nonessential contractor personnel. Determine thresholds and redlines for the evaluation of contractor support. Develop a list of critical contractor positions that must be retained in the event of evacuation. These requirements must be clearly stipulated in the contract language.

15. Develop risk criteria, assessment, and mitigation procedures for contractor movement and operations.

16. Work with the acquisition and legal team to develop flexible statements of work that provide necessary leeway with regard to work hours and that allow for modifications to mission-support requirements during unplanned contingency operations of variable duration and changing environmental conditions.

17. Determine what special contract-administrative functions, surveillance, and managerial controls are required for limited-support environments. Consider how appropriate government controls will be exercised over contractor operations.

18. Consider the appropriate ratio of contractors to oversight personnel, CORs, and government supervisors. Account for the fact that in some contingency operations contractor personnel may be performing services that border closely on inherently governmental functions or for other reasons require increased government supervision and

scrutiny. These administrative and oversight requirements must be accounted for in the government's planning figures for acquisition-support personnel.

19. Consider what organizations will provide contract-administration personnel for surveillance and oversight functions. Determine if these requirements may be satisfied organically by the agency or requiring activity or if they require supplemental personnel from other organizations.

20. Consider any requirements for unique contractor-training requirements due to environmental conditions. This may include specialized training on emergency first aid; military or relief operations; self-defense and personal protective measures; defensive driving; antiterrorism awareness; nuclear, biological, chemical warfare defense; Law of Land Warfare and Geneva Convention; or regionally focused orientation training on local laws, customs, and language for overseas personnel.

21. Consider the requirements for contractor access to support services such as banking institutions, medical support, psychological services, religious support, or legal advice.

22. Determine any government requirements for maintaining records of contractor emergency data, wills, power of attorney, next of kin, and points of contact, if required. In most cases the vendor will be required to provide this type of human resources support, but in some cases there will be cause for the government to maintain this information for all deployed personnel.

23. Consider any other requirements for locally contracted support such as interpreters and linguistic services, drivers, logistics, and engineering-and-facilities-support personnel.

24. Consider to what degree contractors will be integrated into government operations and how that will affect the routing of tasking and requirements from the government to the contractor workforce. Certain situations may require that a vendor provide a more robust management team to oversee employee operations.

25. Generally speaking, the government does not assume responsibility for ensuring the protection of contract workers from workplace, health, or environmental hazards, but be aware that conditions during contingency-support operations may require differing standards of governmental responsibility due to the nature of the environment. These factors should be taken into consideration during the planning of the acquisition team.

Bibliography

Reference Documents and Publications

A Guide to Best Practices for Contract Administration, Office of Federal Procurement Policy (OFPP) (October 1994). www.arnet.gov/comp/seven_steps/library/OFPP guide-bp.pdf.

Army Acquisition Procedures, Pamphlet 70-3, Department of the Army (2008). www .army.mil/usapa/epubs/pdf/p70_3.pdf.

Army Contingency Contracting Handbook, Department of the Army (2006). acqnet .saalt.army.mil/acqinfo/newafar2/afar1197.htm.

Army Contracting Agency Customer Guide (May 2004). www.aca.army.mil/docs/ Community/aca_cust_guide_04.doc.

Army Material Command Contracting Guide (2003). Document not publicly available. Copy in data file.

Army Operational Plans for Contractor Support on the Battlefield, U.S. Army Audit Agency Report (November 2007). www.aaa.army.mil/AAA/AuditReports--Adobe/ 08%20REPORTS/A-2008-0021-FFS%20Army%20Operational%20Plans%20for% 20Contractor%20Support%20on%20the%20Battlefield.pdf.

Best Practices Commercial Quality Assurance Practices Offer Improvements for DOD, Government Accountability Office (1996). www.fas.org/man/gao/ns96162.htm.

Civilian Contractors on the Battlefield, USAWC Strategic Studies Institute Research Paper, Susan Foster (1998). stinet.dtic.mil/cgi-bin/GetTRDoc?AD=ADA346330& Location=U2&doc=GetTRDoc.pdf.

Civilianizing the Force: Is The United States Crossing the Rubicon? Air Force Law Review, Major Michael E. Guillory. afls14.jag.af.mil/JAG_School/The%20Air%20Force%20 Law%20Review/Volume%2051%20(2001)/Civilianizing%20The%20Force_%20Is% 20the%20United%20States%20Crossing%20the%20Rubicon_.doc.

Commercial Augmentation for Intelligence Operations: Lessons Learned from the Global War on Terrorism, Defense Acquisition Review Journal, Glenn Voelz (December 2007). www.dau.mil/pubs/arq/2008arq/ARJ46Web/arq2008_46.asp.

Competencies for the Project Manager, Federal Acquisition Institute Project Managers Competencies Blueprint. www.fai.gov/certification/entry.asp.

Contingency Contracting: A Handbook for the Air Force CCO, Air Force Logistics Management Agency (2003). www.aflma.hq.af.mil/lgj/contingency%20Contracting%20 Mar03_corrections.pdf.

Contingency Contracting: Strengthening the Tail, BG William Bond, Army Logistician Professional Bulletin of Army Logistics, 31, no. 3 (May–June 1999). www.almc .army.mil/alog/issues/MayJun99/1999may_jun/toc_99mj.pdf.

Contracting for the Rest of Us, Department of the Navy Office of Acquisition and Management (2000). www.acq.osd.mil/dpap/Docs/ctrrestofus.pdf.

Contracting Officer Representative (COR) Handbook, Contracting Center Of Excellence (CCE).

Contracting Officer Representatives: Managing the Government's Technical Experts to Achieve Positive Contract Outcomes, U.S. Merit Systems Protection Board Report: (2005). acc.dau.mil/CommunityBrowser.aspx?id=127834&eid=31438&lang=en-US.

Contracting Officer's Representative (COR) Guide, Army Contracting Agency (January 2005). www.aca.army.mil/docs/Community/COR%20Guide.doc.

Contracting Officer's Representative (COR) Handbook, U.S. Army Research, Development, and Engineering Command Acquisition Center (March 2005). www .rdecom-ac.army.mil/corhandbook.swf.

Contracting Officer's Technical Representative (COTR) Training Blueprint, Federal Acquisition Institute (2003). www.fai.gov/pdfs/corbluebook.pdf.

Contracting Officer's Technical Representative Handbook, Federal Aviation Administration (2007). fast.faa.gov/docs/COTR%20handbook%204-07.doc.

Contracting Support on the Battlefield FM 100-10-2, Department of the Army Field Manual (1999). www.globalsecurity.org/military/library/policy/army/fm/100-10-2/ index.html.

Contracting to Rebuild a Nation: The Roles and Responsibilities of U.S. Contracting Activities in Iraq, USAWC Strategic Studies Institute Research Paper, John McGuiness (2005). www.strategicstudiesinstitute.army.mil/pdffiles/ksil45.pdf.

Contract Management: DOD Vulnerabilities to Contracting Fraud, Waste, and Abuse, Government Accountability Office (2006). www.gao.gov/new.items/d06838r.pdf.

Contractor Deployment Guide, Department of the Army Pamphlet 715-16 (1998). www.army.mil/usapa/epubs/pdf/p715_16.pdf.

Contractors Accompanying the Force, Department of the Army Regulation 715-9 (1999). www.army.mil/usapa/epubs/pdf/r715_9.pdf.

Contractors in the Government Workplace, Department of the Army (March 2004). www .aca.army.mil/Library/Library_files/desk%20guids/ACA%20Contractors%20in%20 Workplace%20FINAL%20March%202004.doc.

Contractors in Zones of Conflict: Backbone or Underbelly? USAWC Strategic Studies Institute Research Paper, Steven Mitchell (2005). www.strategicstudiesinstitute .army.mil/pubs/display-papers.cfm?q=167.

Contractors on the Battlefield, USAWC Strategic Studies Institute Research Paper, Ronda Urey (2005). www.strategicstudiesinstitute.army.mil/pubs/display-papers .cfm?q=17.

Contractors on the Battlefield FM 3-100.21 (100-21), Department of the Army Field Manual (January 2003). www.osc.army.mil/gc/files/fm3_100x21.pdf.

Contractors on the Battlefield Report, Lexington Institute Report (2007). lexingtoninstitute.org/docs/contractors_final.pdf.

Contractor Support in the Theater of Operations: Deskbook Supplement, Department of Defense (March 2001). www.dscp.dla.mil/contract/doc/contractor.doc.

Defense Acquisition: Overview, Issues, and Options for Congress, CRS Report to Congress (updated June 20, 2007). www.fas.org/sgp/crs/natsec/RL34026.pdf.

Defense Acquisitions, Improved Management and Oversight Needed to Better Control DOD's Acquisition of Services, Government Accountability Office (2007). www.gao .gov/new.items/d07832t.pdf.

Defense Contracting: Additional Personal Conflict of Interest Safeguards Needed for Certain DOD Contractor Employees, Government Accountability Office (2008). www .gao.gov/new.items/d08169.pdf.

Defense Contracting: Army Case Study Delineates Concerns with Use of Contractors as Contract Specialists, Government Accountability Office (2008). (www.gao .gov/new.items/d08360.pdf.

Defense Contracting in Iraq: Issues and Options for Congress, CRS Report to Congress (updated January 2008). www.fas.org/sgp/crs/natsec/RL33834.pdf.

Defense Management: DOD Needs to Reexamine Its Extensive Reliance on Contractors and Continue to Improve Management and Oversight, Government Accountability Office (2006). www.gao.gov/new.items/d08572t.pdf.

Defense Outsourcing: The OMB Circular A-76 Policy, CRS Report to Congress (updated June 30, 2005). fas.org/sgp/crs/natsec/RL30392.pdf.

DOD Acquisitions: Contracting for Better Outcomes, Government Accountability Office (2006). www.gao.gov/new.items/d06800t.pdf.

Ethics and Procurement Integrity: What You Need to Know as a Federal Employee Involved in the Procurement and Acquisition Process, Office of Government Ethics (2007). www.usoge.gov/pages/forms_pubs_otherdocs/fpo_files/booklets/ bkprocurementintegrity_07.pdf.

The Fisher Report: Effectively Managing Professional Services Contracts: 12 Best Practices, IBM Center for the Business of Government (2006). www.businessofgovernment .org/pdfs/FisherReport.pdf.

The Future of Procurement Workforce: Best Practices in Contracting Lessons Learned from Both a Civilian and Military Standpoint. GovernmentExecutive.com Leadership Breakfast Multimedia Presentation. www.govexec.com/multimedia/ ?sid=51&channel=2.

Glossary of Acquisition Terms, Federal Acquisition Institute. www.fai.gov/pdfs/glossary .pdf.

Glossary of Defense Acquisition Acronyms and Terms, Defense Acquisition University (2005). www.dau.mil/pubs/glossary/preface.asp.

Going to War with Defense Contractors: A Case Study Analysis of Battlefield Acquisition, Air Force Institute of Technology Thesis, Ryan M. Novak (2008). research .maxwell.af.mil/papers/ay2004/afit/AFIT-GAQ-ENV-04M-08.pdf.

Guidance on Receptions, Parties, and Gift Exchanges Involving Coworkers, Contractors, and Supervisors. DOD Standards of Conduct Office, Office of General Counsel. www .dod.mil/dodgc/defense_ethics/dod_oge/DoD_Guidance_Holiday_Parties.doc.

Guidebook for Performance-Based Services Acquisition (PBSA), U.S. Department of Defense (2000). acquisition.gov/comp/seven_steps/library/DODguidebook-pbsa.pdf.

Guidelines for Dealing with Industry, Army Contracting Agency (March 2004). www .aca.army.mil/docs/Community/aca_indstry_gd.doc.

Handbook for Preparation of Statement of Work, U.S. Department of Defense (1991). www.arnet.gov/comp/seven_steps/library/DODhandbook.pdf.

How Should the Army Use Contractors on the Battlefield? Assessing Comparative Risk in Sourcing Decisions, Rand Corporation (2005). rand.org/pubs/monographs/ 2005/RAND_MG296.pdf.

Improved Insight and Controls Needed over DOD's Time-and-Materials Contracts, Government Accountability Office (2007). www.gao.gov/new.items/d07273.pdf.

Increasing Reliance on Contractors on the Battlefield: How Do We Keep from Crossing the Line? Stephen M. Blizzard, Air Force Journal of Logistics (Spring 2004) www .aflma.hq.af.mil/lgj/Afjlhome.html.

Independent Government Cost Estimate (IGCE) Guide, Army Contracting Agency. acc .dau.mil/GetAttachment.aspx?id=31479&pname=file&lang=en-US&aid=5705.

Industry Study: Privatized Military Operations, National Defense University, Industrial College of the Armed Forces (2007). www.ndu.edu/icaf/industry/reports/2007/ pdf/2007_PMOIS.pdf.

Iraq Reconstruction: Lessons in Contracting and Procurement, Special Inspector General for Iraq Reconstruction (July 2006). www.sigir.mil/reports/lessons.aspx.

Joint Contracting Command Iraq (JCC-I) Customer Handbook (2006). Document not publicly available. Copy in data file.

Managing the Private Spies: Use of Commercial Augmentation for Intelligence Operations, Glenn Voelz, Center for Strategic Intelligence Research (2006). www.ndic .edu/press/press.htm.

Military Operations, High-Level DOD Action Needed to Address Long-Standing Problems with Management and Oversight of Contractors Supporting Deployed Forces, Government Accountability Office (2006). www.gao.gov/new.items/d07145.pdf.

Operationalizing Contingency Contracting: Considerations for Effective and Efficient Management of Contingency Contractors during Deployments, USAWC Strategic Studies Institute Paper, Carl Lipsit (2005). www.strategicstudiesinstitute.army .mil/pubs/display-papers.cfm?q=63.

Partnering for Success: A Blueprint for Promoting Government-Industry Communication and Teamwork, U.S. Army Material Command. www.amc.army.mil/amc/ command_counsel/partnering.html.

"Planning: The Key to Contractors on the Battlefield," David L. Young, *Army Logistician Professional Bulletin of Army Logistics* 31, no. 3 (May–June 1999). www .almc.army.mil/ALOG/issues/MayJun99/MS344.htm.

Report of the Acquisition Advisory Panel to the Office of Federal Procurement Policy and the United States Congress (January 2007). acquisition.gov/comp/aap/finalaapreport .html.

Report of the Acquisition Advisory Panel to the Office of Federal Procurement Policy and the United States Congress (January 2007). acquisition.gov/comp/aap/finalaapreport .html.

Report on Competencies for the Contracting Officer's Technical Representative (COTR) Job Function (2003), Submitted to the Federal Acquisition Institute, Office of Government-wide Policy, General Services Administration (2003). www.fai.gov/ pdfs/12-15-03COTRReportFINAL.pdf.

Secure Environment Contracting, Department of the Army Regulation 715-30 (2000). www.fas.org/irp/doddir/army/ar715-30.pdf.

Testimony before the Committee on Homeland Security and Governmental Affairs Subcommittees, U.S. Senate: Military Operations: Implementation of Existing Guidance and Other Actions Needed to Improve DOD's Oversight and Management of Contractors in Future Operations, Government Accountability Office (2006). www.gao .gov/htext/d08436t.html.

Testimony before the Subcommittee on Government Management, Organization, and Procurement, Committee on Oversight and Government Reform, House of Representatives: Federal Contracting: Use of Contractor Performance Information, Government Accountability Office (2007). www.gao.gov/new.items/d071111t.pdf.

Urgent Reform Required: Army Expeditionary Contracting: Report of the Commission on Army Acquisition and Program Management in Expeditionary Operations (2007). www.army.mil/docs/Gansler_Commission_Report_Final_071031.pdf.

U.S. Air Force Guide for the Government-Contractor Relationship (October 2006).

Web Resources

A-76 Competitive Sourcing Internet Library & Directory, www.dla.mil/j-3/a-76/ A-76Main.html.

Acquisition Advisory Panel, www.acquisition.gov/comp/aap/index.html.

Acquisition Central, www.arnet.gov/.

Acquisition Community Connection (ACC), Contracting Communities of Interest, acc .dau.mil/CommunityBrowser.aspx.

Acquisition Knowledge Sharing System (AKSS), deskbook.dau.mil/jsp/default.jsp.

Air Force Acquisition, www.safaq.hq.af.mil/index-2.html.

Air Force Journal of Logistics, www.aflma.hq.af.mil/lgj/Afjlhome.html.

Army Material Command (AMC), Acquisition and Contracting Policy Acquisition Tools, www.amc.army.mil/amc/rda/rda-ap/aqntools.html.

Army Material Command (AMC), Contracting for Best Value: A Best Practices Guide to Source Selection, www.amc.army.mil/amc/rda/rda-ap/ssrc/ssp_toc.htm.

Army Material Command Frequently Asked Questions about Contractors and Contracting, www.amc.army.mil/amc/rda/rda-ac/ck/faq.doc.

Contracting Officer's Representative (COR) Community of Interest, acc.dau.mil/cor.

Contractor on the Battlefield Resource Library, www.afsc.army.mil/gc/battle2.asp.

Contract Specialist Training Blueprints, Federal Acquisition Institute. www.fai.gov/ training/blueprints.asp.

Defense Acquisition Guidebook, akss.dau.mil/dag/DoD5000.asp?view=document.

Defense Acquisition Regulations System, www.acq.osd.mil/dpap/dars/.

Defense Acquisition University, www.dau.mil/.

Defense Acquisition University Virtual Library, www.dau.mil/library/.

Defense FAR Supplement, deskbook.dau.mil/jsp/default.jsp.

Defense Federal Acquisition Regulation Supplement (DFARS) and Procedures, Guidance, and Information (PGI), www.acq.osd.mil/dpap/dars/dfarspgi/current/index.html.

Defense Procurement and Acquisition Policy (DPAP), www.acq.osd.mil/dpap/.

Department of Defense Under Secretary of Defense for Acquisition, Technology and Logistics, ACQWeb, Federal Acquisition Institute. www.fai.gov/index.asp.

Department of the Navy Acquisition One Source, acquisition.navy.mil/content/view/ full/139.

Directorate for Information Operations and Reports: DOD Inspector General Website, www.dodig.osd.mil/index.html.

DOD Annual Report to Congress: Chapter 18: Acquisition Reform (1998), www.dod .mil/execsec/adr98/chap18.html.

DOD Contracting Regulations, www.acq.osd.mil/dpap/dars/index.html.

DTIC (Defense Technical Information Center), www.dtic.mil/.

Ethics Training, www.usoge.gov/pages/comp_web_trng/comp_web_trng_pg2 .html#ogewrkctr_07.

FAR, Circulars, and Supplements, www.arnet.gov/far/.

Federal Acquisition Jumpstation, prod.nais.nasa.gov/pub/fedproc/home.html.

Federal Acquisition Regulation (FAR), www.arnet.gov/far/.

Government Accountability Office (GAO), www.gao.gov/.

Joint Contingency Contracting Handbook, acc.dau.mil/CommunityBrowser .aspx?id=168819&lang=en-US.

Managing, Deploying, Sustaining, and Protecting Contractors on the Battlefield, Joe A. Fortner, www.almc.army.mil/ALOG/issues/SepOct00/MS571.htm.

National Archives and Records Administration, Code of Federal Regulations (Title 48 Federal Acquisition Regulations System), www.access.gpo.gov/cgi-bin/cfrassemble .cgi?title=200548.

Office of Federal Procurement Policy (OFPP): A Guide to Best Practices for Contract Administration, www.acqnet.gov/bestpractices/bestpcont.html.

Office of Federal Procurement Policy (OFPP): Best Practices for Multiple Award Task and Delivery Order Contracting, www.whitehouse.gov/omb/procurement/inter agency_acq/best_practices_multiple_award_task_contracting.html.

Office of Management and Budget, Federal Acquisition Regulatory Council, www .whitehouse.gov/omb/procurement/far/far_council.html.

Office of Management and Budget, Office of Federal Procurement Policy, www .whitehouse.gov/omb/procurement/mission.html.

Performance-Based Service Contracting, www.whitehouse.gov/omb/procurement/pbsa/ guide_pbsc.html.

Regulatory Reform Recommendations of the National Performance Review, www
.piercelaw.edu/risk/vol6/spring/lubbers.htm.

U.S. Army Logistics Management College, www.almc.army.mil/.

*U.S. Department of Energy Environment, Safety and Health (NEPA) Contracting Reform
Guidance and Model SOW,* www.eh.doe.gov/nepa/tools/guidance/con_ref.htm.

U.S. Army Contracting Agency, www.aca.army.mil/.

Index

About the Author

Glenn J. Voelz is an intelligence officer in the United States Army. His recent military assignments include several positions in the Directorate for Intelligence on the Joint Chiefs of Staff at the Pentagon. Previously he served as senior intelligence advisor to the Saudi Arabian Ministry of Defense and assistant professor of history at the United States Military Academy at West Point. During his career he has managed government-contractor workforces for the Department of Defense and Intelligence Community. Lieutenant Colonel Voelz is author of *Managing the Private Spies: The Use of Commercial Augmentation for Intelligence Operations*, as well as several recent articles dealing with contracting issues and intelligence community policy. Lieutenant Colonel Voelz is a graduate of the United States Military Academy at West Point and holds masters degrees from the University of Virginia and the National Defense Intelligence College in Washington, D.C. He is currently assigned to the White House Situation Room.

Breinigsville, PA USA
11 March 2010
234016BV00004B/2/P

9 781605 906980